A LOVE TO DIE FOR

Patricia Springer

Pinnacle Books
Kensington Publishing Corp.
http:www.pinnaclebooks.com

Some names have been changed to protect the privacy of individuals connected to this story.

PINNACLE BOOKS are published by

Kensington Publishing Corp.
850 Third Avenue
New York, NY 10022

Copyright © 2000 by Patricia Springer

All rights reserved. No part of this book may be reproduced in any form or by any means without the prior written consent of the Publisher, excepting brief quotes used in reviews.

If you purchased this book without a cover, you should be aware that this book is stolen property. It was reported as "unsold and destroyed" to the Publisher and neither the Author nor the Publisher has received any payment for this "stripped book."

Pinnacle and the P logo Reg. U.S. Pat. & TM Off.

First Printing: March, 2000
10 9 8 7

Printed in the United States of America

"SHUT UP, YOU BITCH!"

Christa Pike slammed her fists into Colleen Slemmer's head. Then grabbing a handful of hair, she snapped her head backward and then forward down into her knee smashing Colleen's nose. Pike pushed her to the ground, one swift kick after another finding its mark on the nineteen-year-old's body as she begged for it to stop.

Obsessed with her anger, Christa took Colleen's head in both her hands, then slammed her face into the hard ground. Unable to escape the continued blows, Slemmer rolled into a ball, then reached up to grab Pike's arm as she saw the gleam of a blade emerge from her pocket. Christa's hand swept across Colleen's body.

Blood now dripped from the razor-sharp box cutter. As Pike's anger grew, she sliced Colleen on her belly, breasts, and hands in a flurry of erratic swings. She stopped only long enough to exchange the box cutter for the small meat cleaver she'd brought along.

"Take off your clothes," Pike demanded.

Other books by Patricia Springer

BLOOD RUSH
FLESH AND BLOOD
MAIL ORDER BRIDE

Published by Pinnacle Books

This book is dedicated to the memory of Colleen Slemmer and her loving family.

ACKNOWLEDGMENTS

There are always so many people to thank in the preparation of a story that involves the real lives of people. First, and with the greatest appreciation, I thank May Martinez for sharing her most joyful and most painful memories of her daughter. May is a woman of great strength and determination.

I express my highest gratitude to Janice Norman of the Knox County Criminal Court office and to Shirley Hill. They welcomed me warmly, graciously gave assistance with public files, and even provided a private office to review court transcripts.

Also, many thanks go to Judge Mary Beth Leibowitz for her candor; to Randy York for his enthusiasm and expertise; Melvie Burgess, assistant to Judge Leibowitz for all her help; Peggy Atchley, Senior Victim/Witness Coordinator and the staff at the Tennessee Court of Appeals for their assistance; and John North and Charley Belcher for their reflections.

In the area of technical expertise, I thank James Cron, Certified Latent Print Examiner and Certified Senior Crime Scene Analyst; Greg Miller, Attorney-at-Law; and my good friends and distinguished professionals Tina Church of TC Investigations, and Dr. Melody Milam Potter, Ph.D.

As with any project I undertake, I thank my editorial consultant and friendly "watch dog," LaRee Bryant. Gratitude also to the ever-patient and supportive Karen Haas. I consider both these women not only my right-hand ladies, but my friends.

Prologue

May Martinez's eyes moistened as she watched her daughter fold the last pair of blue jeans and carefully place them in the suitcase lying open on the bed. Nineteen-year-old Colleen brushed her honey-blond hair from her face and smiled at her mother.

"It's only a six-month commitment," Colleen reminded her mother as she tried to hide the excitement in her voice. "I'll be back."

Colleen's reassurance didn't minimize the sense of doom that swallowed May like the blackness of a moonless night. Colleen had never been away from home, and Knoxville, Tennessee, was a long way from Orange Park, Florida—a long way from family and friends. Perhaps that explained the mixture of fear and sadness that churned May's stomach that early morning in September 1994.

As Colleen snapped the latch on the worn suitcase, May felt her heart snap inside her. May closed her eyes momentarily and silently tried to convince herself that it would only be a short time before her child returned. When the mugginess of late summer turned to the crispness of winter, Colleen would be home.

A reading disability had dampened Colleen's enthusiasm for learning. She'd dropped out of school soon after entering the ninth grade. Tired of rolling burritos at Taco Bell and wrapping hamburgers at Wendy's, Colleen realized she wanted more. Just as Colleen was contemplating returning to high school, she learned about the Job Corps where she could get her GED and begin computer training—begin to turn her life around. The Jacksonville, Florida Job Corps recruiter had spoken of opportunity for a new beginning. A chance at a good career. The recruiter had convinced her that the Job Corps was her ticket to success.

Although there was a Job Corps Center in Jacksonville, only a short drive from her Orange Park home, they didn't offer the computer training Colleen desired. Her family could not afford to pay for the special schooling, so she would have to go to a center in Knoxville, Tennessee. In early September 1994, Colleen Slemmer kissed her mother, stepfather, and baby sister good-bye and headed to the rolling hills of Tennessee.

Sitting on the Job Corps bus, Colleen watched as the crowded vehicle sped past the familiar palm trees of Jacksonville. Soon Florida's most populous city would be behind her. She would miss the deepwater harbor lined with high-rise buildings; watching the Annual Mug Race, the longest river sailboat race in the world that runs along the St. Johns River; the roar of the crowd from the annual Gator Bowl football classic; and of course, she would miss her family. Colleen's blue eyes danced with excitement as the familiar sights of Jacksonville faded in the distance. She was embarking on a new adventure, a new beginning.

Colleen's bright eyes dimmed as she stared out the bus window at the bleak Knoxville Job Corps campus. The old converted motel complex was a far cry from the college-style compound she had envisioned. As she walked the halls toward her assigned room, graffiti-defaced walls shouted words of violence, hate—trouble. Colleen's enthusiasm, her expectations for the future, were suddenly saturated by a flood of hostility from her new environment.

Barely three weeks after arriving at the Knoxville Job Corps Center, Colleen telephoned her mother, pleading to return to Orange Park.

"It's so depressing here," Colleen cried. "I hate it! The dormitory walls are painted black and the ceilings are purple."

But it wasn't only the color scheme of the residence hall that disturbed Colleen. Young as she was, she recognized the lack of supervision as a big problem. She hated it when students ran screaming down the halls. And was furious when her room was raided, and clothes and jewelry taken from her. Not only did she call her mother to complain, but the Job Corps counselor as well.

"There are three students who keep stalking me," Colleen grumbled. "They come in my room, take my things, and threaten me. One girl has even come in my room with knives. She thinks I'm after her boyfriend, but I'm not."

May Martinez recognized the fear in her middle daughter's voice, the same unidentified fear she herself had felt the day Colleen packed to leave for Knoxville. May hadn't wanted Colleen to go to the Job Corps in the first place. She had heard that it wasn't very good, but Colleen had been determined to get her GED and become trained in computers. All May could do was encourage Colleen to make the best of the situation. After all, she had signed a contract and would be required to stay for her full commitment.

The Job Corps counselor, on the other hand, didn't seem to think Colleen's complaints were much of a problem. In a patronizing tone he assured Colleen he'd look into the matter, but to Colleen's knowledge nothing had been done. The torment by the trio continued. A trio whom Colleen had failed to identify by name to her worried mother.

Christmas 1994 came as a welcome relief for Colleen. She spent two happy, stress-free weeks with her biological father in Pennsylvania. On January 7, 1995, she called her mother from her dorm in Tennessee.

"I had a great Christmas," she said, the familiar

bubbly excitement back in her voice. "One of the best. Only another month and I'll be home." She was happy to be returning to Florida. Happier still to be leaving the Job Corps.

May breathed a sigh of relief when the conversation was finished. Colleen would soon be safely home.

On January 12 Colleen called again, a breezy, fast call that made May smile. "Not much longer till I see you. Gotta go. I'm going to Blockbuster to pick up a movie. I love you, Mom. 'Bye." May smiled. Colleen seemed to have worked through her problems at the Job Corps. She would have the computer training she wanted.

Two days later there was another call from Knoxville. But this time there was a stranger on the line, Detective Randy York of the Knoxville Police Department. Colleen was dead.

One

The night air was chilled as it blew across the icy waters of the Tennessee River. January in Knoxville could be brutally cold.

Colleen Slemmer pulled the pink, blue, and white sweater her mother had given her for Christmas over her head. She smiled as she tugged her hair from beneath the neck band. The garment, which complimented her fair complexion and accentuated her clear blue eyes, reminded her of her family in Florida. She couldn't wait to get back home. Couldn't wait to leave the Knoxville Job Corps, a place she'd thought would be her salvation. A place she'd come to hate.

After slipping into her jeans, she tied the laces of her white Nike tennis shoes, and carefully adjusted the cuffs of her blue socks. Knowing that it would be cold on the walk from the Job Corps campus to the Blockbuster store, Colleen topped her sweater and jeans with a hunter green wool coat, pulled on black knit gloves, and headed for the parking lot adjacent to the dormitory where she had agreed to meet fellow Job Corps student Christa Pike.

Colleen had wondered if she should go. She and Christa had had their differences the past few months. Colleen nervously tugged at the thin gold chain encircling her slim neck. Something wasn't right. Earlier in the evening Christa had asked her to meet her about 8:00 o'clock and walk to the video store near the campus. It was uncharacteristic of Christa to be nice to Colleen. After all, Christa had angrily accused Colleen of trying to steal her boyfriend, Tadaryl Shipp, and had often made rude comments to Colleen about it. Even though Colleen had assured Christa she wasn't interested in Tadaryl, there had been friction between the two for some time. Christa had started rumors about Colleen and had even picked a fight with her on the Job Corps grounds. Today, Christa seemed different. Her attitude was congenial, even friendly. Perhaps she had finally accepted that Colleen wasn't attracted to her boyfriend.

Colleen shook off the feeling of uneasiness that had crept over her as she headed for the parking lot. She had just returned from a wonderful trip to see her father and nothing was going to bring her down.

Colleen was surprised, and somewhat relieved, to see Tadaryl Shipp and Shadolla Peterson waiting with Christa. Tadaryl's coarse, bushy hair had recently been brushed free of the tight braids Shadolla occasionally tied for him. His full upper lip was outlined by a thin dark mustache. Shadolla's hair was pulled back on the right, with tight braids falling to her chin, casually framing the left side of her face. Her full lips and large, dark eyes were prominent features of her oval-shaped face.

Colleen knew the two African Americans were friends of Christa's, but she hadn't expected the two Job Corps students to go along with them to Blockbuster. She felt more relaxed with the additional company. Little did Colleen know that Christa's plan was to lure Colleen to a deserted section of the University of Tennessee Agriculture Campus to teach her a lesson.

Tadaryl had originally planned on remaining at the Job Corps Center while Shadolla and Christa confronted "the little whore," as Christa referred to Colleen. He feared something bad might happen to Christa when she challenged Colleen, so he changed his mind and signed out of the Job Corps along with Christa and Shadolla.

Colleen smiled broadly as she greeted the three in the parking lot, exposing a slight chip in her right front tooth. Her thin-lipped grin emphasized her high cheekbones and sparkling blue eyes. She was a pretty girl.

In contrast to Colleen's heart-shaped face, Christa had an innocent, round, baby face that concealed the hard times of her troubled youth. Her sad eyes revealed a girl filled with years of sorrow. Christa's dark, natural curls, unlike Colleen's medium-length, light brown hair, were wild and untamed. The girls' physical appearances were as different as their personalities.

"I have some weed hidden up at Tyson Park," Christa said as they turned onto Cumberland Avenue, known to locals as "the strip" because of its proximity to the University of Tennessee. "We can go up there and have a smoke." Christa's high voice with its distinctive Southern drawl was nonthreatening.

Colleen felt a bit less reluctant to accompany the trio to the popular local park. With little more than a month to go before she left for home, she thought that this might be her only chance to clear the air with Christa. Maybe her final month with the Corps could be more peaceful than the last few had been. She fell in beside Tadaryl, who was walking about three feet ahead of Christa and Shadolla. They passed the University of Tennessee campus, traveled under the railroad viaduct, and between the dual signs that marked the entrance to Tyson Park.

Tadaryl led the others as they split the red brick sign on the right and a wooden sign on the left. Set in the brick wall was an open invitation to the public area.

TYSON PARK

THIS PARK FOR THE USE OF ALL THE
PEOPLE OF KNOXVILLE WAS GIVEN BY
GEN. LAURANCE DAVIS TYSON, D.S.M.
AND HIS WIFE,
BETTIE MCGHEE TYSON

The worn wooden structure on the left also bore the name of the park. A round emblem designating the area as part of the Knoxville Parks and Recreation department was attached in the upper left corner, and a small square sign announcing Tyson Park as a bird sanctuary adorned the bottom right.

Colleen's eyes fell on the hours of operation painted in white on the plank structure. Colleen read 9:00 A.M. TILL 9:00 P.M. They wouldn't have much time.

From the main park road, the students turned onto the bike path that wound seven miles throughout the park area. As they passed the covered picnic tables and stepped onto the wooden bridge crossing over Third Creek, Colleen pulled the collar of her green coat tighter to her throat. The winter air was as biting as the shallow, icy water running swiftly beneath the wood-plank bridge.

The farther they trekked into the park, the darker the night became. Tadaryl and Shadolla's dark skin melted into the backdrop of the moonlit sky, while Christa's and Colleen's pale white faces glimmered in the occasional beam of car lights above them on Cumberland Avenue. Although Colleen couldn't see Christa's dark eyes dance with excitement as she whispered secretively to Shadolla, her feeling of uneasiness returned.

The four students walked single file through a darkened tunnel that led them dangerously close to the freezing waters of the fast-running creek.

Colleen's feet slid on the slick, mossy walkway, habitually damp from creek water lapping over the bank's low edge. Although the near slip made her smile, she couldn't shake her anxiety.

"Damn, how much farther is it?" Colleen asked nervously.

"You'll see," Christa responded with a giggle of anticipation.

She was proud of herself. Proud that she'd managed to lure Colleen to that dark, remote area. An area so secluded that someone wasn't likely to hear words—or screams.

With the smokestacks at the University of Tennessee power plant looming over their path, Colleen finally confronted Christa. "There isn't any weed up here, is there, Christa?" Colleen asked with an indignant air.

"No, there isn't," Christa answered, a smirk tilting her plump lips.

"Then why did you bring me up here?" Colleen demanded, trying to keep a quaver out of her voice.

"I just want to talk to you and find out what's going on. I want the truth. I want you to tell me why you're doing all this stuff to me. Why did you call me a 'nigger lovin' whore'? You know I've been under a lot of stress. I don't know why you keep trying to do things to bug me. Trying to take Tadaryl away from me. Trying to get me in trouble. I can't handle it anymore." Christa's dark curls vibrated as she shook her head in obvious frustration.

"You bitch!" Colleen shouted.

Suddenly Colleen's head jerked to the right as Christa's fist connected with Colleen's left cheek. Colleen's ears rang. Again and again, Christa's knuckles pounded against the other girl's skull.

"Please stop! Please stop!" Colleen begged, trying to cover her face and head with her arms.

"I don't appreciate everything you've been doing to me. Why do you keep on being such a smart ass?" Christa asked angrily, striking another blow.

Colleen took a quick step back from her aggressor. Anger filled her eyes. Reckless fire brewed in her belly. "Because I can. And because I want to," she fired back. "Is this why you brought me up here? Just to do this?"

"Yeah!" Christa shouted. "I want to know what's going on. I'm so mad right now that I can't even see straight. I can't fight you at the Job Corps Center or I'll get terminated. I can't afford that." The eighteen-year-old's eyes narrowed, her rage heightened by Colleen's rebellious spirit.

Tadaryl stood beside Shadolla a few feet from where Colleen and Christa were arguing. His black T-shirt, nylon jogging pants, and hooded sweatshirt helped him blend further into the night. Only the occasional sparkle of the five-pointed pentagram medallion he wore around his neck broke the ebony image.

Colleen's angry voice shattered the momentary silence between the female adversaries. "You bitch!" she shouted again. Fury filled the void inside her, where fear had been only moments earlier.

Shadolla stood motionless, except for her fingers nervously twisting the narrow braids that draped the left side of her face. Her eyes were expressionless as she watched her friend's face fill with brutal indignation.

Christa readied herself for battle. She slammed her fists into Colleen's head again. Then she grabbed a handful of Colleen's hair, snapped her head backward, and with the same quick speed, pushed Colleen's face down toward her knee.

Colleen screamed as her nose smashed into the denim fabric of Christa's Guess jeans. She clung to her attacker, pulling at her arms, clinging to her legs.

"Don't touch me!" Christa screamed. "I don't want you to touch me! I can't stand it!"

Christa pushed Colleen to the pebbled ground. One swift kick after another found its mark on Colleen's body. Tears spilled from Colleen's eyes as she begged again and again for Christa to stop.

Obsessed with anger, Christa took Colleen's head in both hands, lifted it slightly, then slammed her suspected rival's face into the hard ground.

"Why are you doing this to me?" Colleen whimpered.

"I know all the stuff you've been sayin' to Tadaryl. I know all the stuff you are sayin' about me and about a lot of other people on campus.

I don't know why you're doin' it. All you're doin' is makin' me mad," Christa answered, sneering down at the battered girl lying at her feet.

Tadaryl kept his distance, simply watching as the two young women battled. Battled over him. Feeling smug, special, the seventeen-year-old made no move to stop the intensity of Christa's attack on Colleen.

Finding renewed strength, Colleen yelled, "Fuck you! Just fuck you! You can't do this to me. You're going to get terminated from the program anyway, and I'm going to get my friend to jump on you. You bitch!"

"Shut up!" Christa shouted as she kicked Colleen in the face.

Blood spurted from Colleen's cheek and filled her mouth with its metallic taste. Unable to escape the continued blows, she rolled into a ball, covering her head with her slender arms. Colleen gasped for air between painful sobs. Then, with one last surge from somewhere deep inside her, Colleen managed to get to her feet and run. A desperate attempt at escape.

As Colleen fled from her attacker, unexpectedly her legs gave way to something blocking her path. She stumbled and went crashing to the ground, water from a puddle beneath her spraying her clothes. She looked up to see Tadaryl standing over her. The questions in her tear-filled eyes were obvious: Why? Why had he tripped her? Why didn't he help her escape the insanity of Christa Pike?

"Bang her head on the ground. Knock her unconscious," Christa demanded.

Tadaryl didn't hesitate. In response to Christa's demands, he pushed Colleen's head into the ground with all the strength he could muster. More tears filled her eyes, glistening on her cheeks as she looked up at him and whispered, "Why?" Moments later, she lay motionless. Her breathing was ragged, her body moving up and down with each exhausted gasp.

Colleen again tried to escape; Tadaryl and Christa jumped to hold her down. Colleen clawed the ground in a desperate attempt to flee. With Christa holding one leg and Tadaryl the other, they dragged Colleen Slemmer's struggling body down the path, closer to some dense underbrush.

As Colleen continued to fight for freedom, Christa's anger intensified. She plunged her hand deep into the pocket of her black, bomber-style, leather jacket. A snippet of silver glistened in the dim light as Christa's hand emerged from her pocket. Colleen reached up to grab Christa's arm. Instinctively, Christa's head jerked backward as the blade of the knife came dangerously close to her own pale, round face.

"She almost made me cut my face!" Christa exclaimed, fear mixing with anger in her voice. Then, almost as a reflex, Christa's hand swept across Colleen's body.

Colleen cried out in excruciating agony and clutched her stomach. Blood spilled onto the pink and blue flowers of her new sweater. And blood dripped from the razor-sharp box cutter in Christa Pike's hand. Colleen continued to scream in pain as Christa stood over her, staring at the blood seeping from her enemy's body.

Shadolla's eyes widened. She knew Christa had intended to teach Colleen a lesson. She had even known she'd brought the box cutter just to scare the girl. But the situation was out of control. Christa had gone too far.

"She's going to tell on you! You're going to go to prison! You've got to do something!" Shadolla yelled frantically as she stared at the bloody box cutter in Christa's hand. "If you let her go, she's going to go back, and you're going to be in deep shit, Christa. You gotta do something! You got to do something so she can't tell on you! Don't let her get up and go tell on you!"

Christa knew it was true. This was no longer intimidation and revenge. This was attempted murder. She didn't dare let Colleen live.

While Christa contemplated her next move, Colleen found renewed purpose, got to her feet, and again tried to run for her life. But Christa wasn't far behind. The young teen reached down, picked up a good-sized rock, and hurled it at her rival. The rock hit with a heavy thud and Colleen fell to the ground. Again, she tried to rise and run. Again, she was knocked down and her abused body dragged back to the bushes where the attack initially began.

"Can I talk to you?" Colleen asked in desperation. "Christa, can I talk to you?"

"What would you have to say to me now?" Christa sneered.

"Somebody out of Teresa's group is after Tadaryl."

"No, they're not," Christa said, dismissing Colleen's statement. "You don't know what you're talking about. You're sitting here trying to get out of this because you know it's went too far."

"Wait, wait," Colleen pleaded, her voice a mere whisper. "Just hear me out for a minute. Just let me get up. I'll walk to Florida. I'll walk home. I won't go back and say anything about you all. I promise."

Colleen's frantic ramblings continued. She wanted to live. She begged to live.

"Bitch, you're stupid!" Christa sneered. "I don't want to talk to you. I don't want you to talk to me. I just want to find some way to get out of this. It's gone too far. I didn't mean to do what I've done so far, but it's too late now. It's just something that happened. I'm not about to let you go from here and tell on me and me be in a big shit load of trouble. Now, I'm going to be rotting in prison because of your stupid ass."

Christa was down in Colleen's face, her anger escalating. She began wielding her weapon in a flurry of erratic swings, slicing Colleen on belly and breasts and hands.

"Let me up," Colleen desperately pleaded. "I'll walk to Florida. I'll leave right now and won't even take any of my clothes or nothin'."

"Shut up!" Christa ordered her, emphasizing

her command with a swift kick to Colleen's face. But Colleen would not shut up. She continued to talk. Continued to plead for her life.

"Take off your clothes," Christa demanded, hoping that Colleen would stop trying to run away if she were nude.

Reluctantly, Colleen removed her coat. She sat motionless, staring at Christa, her eyes desperate and bewildered. When Colleen hesitated to remove her sweater, Tadaryl stepped forward to yank the garment over her head. Colleen's coat was tossed high in the branches of a nearby tree and her sweater flung into the thick undergrowth a few feet below the coat. She did not remove her bloodstained jeans, shoes, or socks.

Colleen shivered in the cold. Her bra hung off one arm, the strap cut by one of the many slashes. Bloody, bruised, she lay in the dirt, sheltered by the outstretched arms of an oak tree. She was weak from the loss of blood and from the savage blows she'd endured, but she was relentless in her quest for freedom.

Christa could see Colleen's mouth moving, but couldn't hear the words. Her anger had consumed her, taken over her senses. She felt as though her body had been lifted above the other three in the clearing. It was as though she had become an observer to the actions taking place in front of her.

An unfamiliar noise a short distance down the path sent panic surging through Christa.

"Wait, I think I hear something," Christa whispered harshly.

She stepped away from her victim and walked a few feet down the darkened roadway. The area was littered with old building materials, large pieces of plastic, and chunks of used asphalt. The smokestacks loomed high above her like incriminating fingers pointing to the heavens.

"Nobody's there," she told Tadaryl on her return.

Still high on the violence, he began screaming obscenities at Colleen.

Despite all she'd endured, Colleen struggled to gain her balance, obviously determined to run yet again.

But Christa had other plans. She reached into her jacket pocket and produced another weapon, one borrowed from a friend at the dorm. Seconds later, Colleen's pained voice shrilled loudly as Christa slashed her with a small meat cleaver. Blood seeped from a gash that started at her left shoulder, and angled diagonally down toward her right hip. Christa Pike stood behind her, the bloody cleaver gripped tightly in her right hand. But not even that terrible wound kept Colleen from trying to escape. Once more, she tried to run. Once more, she was knocked to the ground and dragged back to the bushes.

Christa's anger continued to rage as Colleen beseeched her assailant to show mercy. Nothing she said slowed her attacker. Christa reached down, tugged on the muddy blue-jean fabric covering Colleen's upper right thigh, less than an inch from her crotch, and taunted Colleen.

"You could lose this if you don't use it right," Christa said, referring to Colleen's sexuality.

Colleen held her breath as she heard the steel blade rip through the heavy, bloodstained denim fabric.

"I heard you say you wanted to fuck him. I was standing around the corner when you said it. I love him to death," Christa declared. "I mean, I really do."

"Why are you doing this to me? I told you I'm not interested in Tadaryl!" Tears streamed down Colleen's face.

Colleen's words went unheeded. Christa was far past any chance of hearing. She wasn't going to lose another person she loved . . . no matter what it took.

With one vicious swipe of the box cutter, Christa cut a huge gash across Colleen's throat.

"That should shut her up," Christa muttered under her breath.

But she was wrong. Colleen continued to whine. To beg.

Christa ripped the scrap of white cloth she had used earlier in the evening to tie back her own hair and began wrapping it around Colleen's open mouth. Tadaryl knotted the rag tightly. Again, Colleen instinctively grabbed at Christa's hands and tried to speak.

"Stop that!" Christa screamed over the moaning of her victim "And shut up! I don't want to hear you talk.'

Fear and frailty halted Colleen's pleadings and her struggle for freedom. She sat silently, her hands folded obediently in her lap as Christa finished tying the torn piece of bed sheet around her mouth. Strands of Colleen's hair, stained with bright red blood, protruded from the knot of the cloth.

Moving in closer to the girls, Tadaryl took the box cutter from Christa's hand. Leaning over Colleen's bare, bloody chest, he listened momentarily to the girl's labored, gurgling breathing. Then, swiftly, he cut the midsection of her bra, both sides falling away to reveal her breasts. Meticulously, Tadaryl sliced Colleen's chest, while muffled whimpers came from the near-nude young woman. Standing back, he admired his carving— a pentagram, just like the ones he and Christa wore around their necks. He then took two or three more swipes at Colleen with the cutter, slashing her neck this time.

Christa reclaimed the box cutter from Tadaryl and cut a circle around the pentagram figure. She looked into Tadaryl's deep, dark eyes, a smile on her lips. Then she turned to stare at Colleen Slemmer, bloody, dirty, and gasping for air in a pool of her own blood. As if in response to Tadaryl's icon, Christa cut a five-pointed star in Colleen's forehead.

Colleen was breathing blood in and out of her rapidly filling lungs and her body made small, rapid jerking movements.

The lurching and twitching of her victim's body irritated Christa even more. She resumed beating Colleen's head with her fists and kicking her battered body. The gag across Colleen's mouth slipped to her neck, quickly absorbing the rapid flow of blood from the multiple neck wounds. Colleen remained silent.

Christa bent down closer to her victim, her mouth only inches from Colleen's bloody ear. "Colleen, do you know what's doing this to you?" Christa asked. Colleen only moaned. Christa smiled, knowing that Colleen understood that it was she who had inflicted the pain. She who had administered the torture. She who had won.

Except, Colleen was still alive.

Christa couldn't believe her hated rival was still breathing. For almost an hour she had tortured Colleen Slemmer. Cut her. Beaten her. Savagely mutilated her. What would it take to kill her?

Tadaryl had the answer to Christa's question. He handed her a large piece of broken roadway asphalt. Christa lifted the jagged chunk over her head. Tadaryl couldn't watch; he'd seen enough. He turned away from the gory scene. Clouded by tears and pain, Colleen Slemmer's blue eyes watched in horror as Christa plunged the asphalt mass downward toward her head. She couldn't speak. She couldn't raise her arms to stop the final attack. Weak from loss of blood and her vehement fight for her life, she simply lay there . . . helpless to stop Christa.

Jealousy had captured Christa's soul. Again and

again, she lifted the rock and slammed it into Colleen's skull until the asphalt split the hard bone into two pieces.

"Stop, Christa! That's enough!" Tadaryl called.

"No, I want to see brains."

So, with all the force she could gather, Christa hit Colleen one last time. "There they go." Christa smiled in satisfaction as she watched a gray liquid ooze from Colleen's head.

"La, la, la, la, la," Christa sang as she danced around her victim's body.

Colleen Slemmer was finally silenced. No more whimpers. No more begging.

No more threat to Christa's happiness.

Two

Tadaryl Shipp and Christa Pike dragged Colleen Slemmer's limp body through the mud one final time.

"I can't drag her anymore," Tadaryl said, panting heavily. "I'm about to have an asthma attack."

Christa attempted to drag the one-hundred-and-ten-pound woman by herself, then stopped abruptly. "She's all gooey. I don't want to touch her anymore."

Colleen's legs rested on the uphill side of a refuse bank of discarded roadway materials, next to the tree where her coat and sweater had been tossed earlier.

Christa's body shook with short, rapid breaths. She pushed her sweat-dampened hair from her face and stared at Colleen's lifeless body. She barely recognized the person lying on the pile of dirt under the sprawling tree as her classmate. Mud, leaves, and twigs adhered to Colleen's twisted form. She had put up quite a struggle. Christa's eyes glistened as though an amusing thought had come to her. The eighteen-year-old reached down to the shattered skull of her victim. From Colleen's matted hair, now red with blood, Christa picked out a small piece of bone. A fragment of Colleen's skull.

"Look what I have. I have a souvenir," she said, grinning broadly as she slipped the piece of bone into the pocket of her jacket.

"It's a full moon outside, and you know what that means," Tadaryl said, returning Christa's smile, "Tomorrow is Friday the thirteenth, my father's birthday."

Shadolla shot a questioning look at Tadaryl.

"Satan's birthday," he explained.

Christa and Tadaryl walked to a nearby mud puddle, down slope from where Colleen's body rested. They washed Colleen's blood from their hands, and Christa made a feeble attempt to wash the red stains from her tennis shoes.

Then the trio walked in silence, retracing their steps through Tyson Park, back toward the Job Corps campus. They stopped at a Texaco along the strip, hoping to wash away more of Colleen's blood from their clothing.

Standing in the small, hazily lit restroom, Christa removed her blue-and-white Fila tennis shoes and began scrubbing the red blood from the crevices of the white leather. The laces were more of a problem. The porous fabric had rapidly absorbed her victim's blood. Now dried, the blood could not be washed away.

Loosening the black leather belt that encircled

her waist, Christa noticed the bloodstains on her Guess jeans. Knowing that any attempt to remove the blood in the washroom sink would be ineffective, she smeared mud from the bottom of her rubber-soled shoes over the blood-soaked areas of her jeans. *That will have to do for now,* she thought. *That should get me back to the Center without somebody noticing.*

But in the dark of Tyson Park and in the low-lit restroom, Christa hadn't noticed the blood splatters on her bomber jacket. The dark stains blended into the black leather like chips of coal on a slag heap.

Once Christa was satisfied that her appearance would go unnoticed, she shoved Colleen's black gloves and three photo-identification cards into the restroom trash can, far below the crumpled paper towels and bits of white toilet tissue. Authorities would have difficulty identifying the mutilated body of Colleen Slemmer without identification.

The three friends walked back down the strip and toward the Job Corps campus in silence. On the outskirts of the campus property, Tadaryl and Christa instructed Shadolla to tell no one what had happened at Tyson Park.

Stunned by the killing, Shadolla nodded in agreement, afraid she would be in danger if she told anyone how Colleen had died.

The trio passed several friends who had congregated in the Job Corps parking lot about ten o'clock. Christa worried whether anyone would notice her appearance.

"What happened to your jeans?" Pasty, a friend of Christa's, asked.

Christa giggled nervously. "Oh I fell in a mud puddle," she said, looking at the mud-smeared legs of her jeans. She moved on to the privacy of her room, removed the soiled garment, turned it inside out, and tucked it above her suitcase at the top of her closet. She showered, changed, and made her way down the hall to return the meat cleaver borrowed from another unsuspecting student.

Christa was still exhilarated from the slaughter of Colleen. She was running high on adrenaline. It was not a time to sleep. She wanted to party. Talk to friends. Brag about her ultimate feat of annihilation.

"Hi, Kim," Christa said as she bounded into Kim Iloilo's second floor room. "I have something to tell you." Christa sat down on the side of Kim's bed. She was smiling and appeared to be very excited about something. "First, you can't say anything."

"Okay," Kim agreed. Her straight hair, dark skin, and Hawaiian features were striking.

"I just killed Colleen Slemmer." Christa's news was delivered matter-of-factly, with a slight tone of self-satisfaction.

"What?" Kim asked, dumbfounded.

Christa was always acting tough, spouting off at the mouth about how mean she was, but never had she rendered such a shocking confession.

"I cut Colleen's throat six times. Tadaryl

helped. I kept cutting her because she wouldn't shut up. I beat her up, and threw asphalt at her head," Christa said, dancing about the room in a small circle while she imitated her actions of a few hours earlier on the desolate university road.

"La, la, la, la, la, la," Christa sang, as she reenacted the dance of death she had performed around Colleen's body.

Kim Iloilo sat speechless on the twin bed. Unable to move. Unable to talk.

Could Christa be telling her the truth? Kim thought back to her conversation with Christa the night before in that very room.

What had Christa said? "I'm going to kill Colleen Slemmer." Kim had asked Christa why, and her friend had only replied, "Because I feel mean today."

Kim hadn't believed her. She thought her friend was just acting thuggish. Just trying to scare Colleen. No one would believe she would really kill someone. Would they?

Then Kim remembered seeing Christa earlier that night. She was looking for Shadolla—"to get a box cutter from her," Kim recalled. Then about 8:15 P.M., she'd watched Christa, Tadaryl, Shadolla, and Colleen leave the campus together. When she saw them again at 10:15 P.M., Christa and Shadolla were alone. She hadn't thought much about it at the time. Colleen and Tadaryl could have come back sooner, or they could still be out. Now Kim questioned if Christa could possibly be telling her the truth.

Christa sat back down on the bed beside Kim. She reached in her pocket and pulled out a small piece of bone.

"It's a piece of Colleen's skull," she said, almost laughing. "A souvenir." She held the fragment as though it was a coveted prize.

Many psychologists would say Christa's actions displayed signs of an organized killer, one who often takes a personal item belonging to the victim as a trophy, or to hinder the police in identifying the victim. Christa had done both: taking, then discarding Colleen's identification cards; and seizing a piece of her victim's skull as a souvenir. Most often organized killers do not take items of intrinsic value, such as expensive jewelry, but, rather, items that are used to recall the victim. Christa would use the piece of Colleen's skull in her post-crime fantasies and to acknowledge her accomplishment. Just as a hunter uses the head of his prey mounted on the wall to take satisfaction in having killed it, Christa would use the piece of bone from Colleen's head to keep alive the excitement of her crime.

Kim's stomach was suddenly queasy. Her head ached. How could this have happened?

Remembering Christa's confession, her promenade around an imaginary body, and the valued treasure she kept close in her pocket, Kim spent a sleepless night. She had to know the truth. Was it just another one of Christa's boastful lies, or was Colleen really dead? Kim was scared. If Christa could kill Colleen with no sign of remorse, could she kill her as well? Kim wished Christa hadn't confided in her. She wished she was back home.

The next morning, Kim met Christa in the school cafeteria for breakfast. "What did you do with the piece of skull?" Kim asked.

"It's in my pocket," Christa answered, taking a bite of eggs. "I'm eating breakfast with it."

Her grin was wide and smug.

Three

University of Tennessee groundskeeper Duncan Sutherland looked closely at the bloody form lying in the dirt and tall grasses on the edge of the UT Agricultural campus.

The fifteen-year UT employee had arrived for work as scheduled, Friday morning, January 13, 1995. After clocking in near the greenhouses at 8:05, he began his morning rounds, policing the area for trash. As Sutherland headed toward the Agriculture Engineering building, a relatively secluded area just past the old steam plant, he spotted an unidentifiable mound among the scrub trees and scruff grasses.

It must be a dog, Sutherland thought. *But that doesn't make any sense.* The early morning shadows obscured his view. Tilting his head to the left, Sutherland studied the figure closely. He couldn't be certain what he was seeing. Slowly, he left the gravel roadway and took several steps toward the lifeless form resting on the man-made embankment. Something caught his eye and he looked to the right, spying an object hanging in a nearby tree. A sweater was snagged in the branches several feet above the ground. He gaped at the sweater for a moment, then noticed a second garment, a green coat about twenty feet higher in the sprawling branches.

This picture isn't right, he thought. He glanced back at what he had first believed to be a dead dog. Cautious, he moved closer and gasped aloud when he realized the blood-soaked bundle wasn't a dog at all—it was a human body. A body riddled with knife wounds.

Sutherland stood frozen to the cold, muddy ground. He was about five feet from the corpse when he realized it was a woman. She lay on her side, and he could see one breast and a large portion of her half-nude, beaten, and slashed torso. Her head was split open and gray matter had spilled onto the ground.

Shock immobilized Sutherland. He remained motionless, scarcely breathing. He didn't want to believe what he was seeing. *Maybe I'm not seeing what I think I see*, Sutherland tried to persuade himself. *This can't be real.*

Reality dawned then and Sutherland ran to a work crew across the street from Morgan Hall, pleading with two plumbers to go back to the area with him.

Officer John Johnson received the first call that there was something unusual spotted near the agricultural campus. He parked his University of

Tennessee patrol car behind the old steam plant at Neyland Drive and Lake Loudon Boulevard and started down to the path. Almost immediately, he saw three men waving their arms, directing him toward them.

"Down here," the men shouted as they motioned the officer to their location. "There's a body down here."

The body was not visible from the Third Creek bike trail. Johnson moved in for a closer examination. He grimaced as he looked at what was left of the face of the partially clad person. Identifying the young female was going to be a challenge. Her head was a mass of blood and hair, her face totally indistinguishable.

"Everyone move back," Johnson ordered. "Move to that area over there." He pointed to a spot just north of the crime scene. The UT employees obeyed without uttering an objection.

The killer, or killers, had made no effort to conceal the body, although discarded plastic and building materials littered the area just behind the old steam plant. Beginning at an old cargo trailer, Johnson immediately began stringing yellow tape around the sector. The stark black words printed on the tape—POLICE DO NOT ENTER—were an unmistakable indication that something very serious had taken place on the tranquil southern campus,

Officer Robert Rector of the Knoxville Police Department arrived and began helping Johnson secure the area. Initially the crime-scene tape encompassed a territory only in the immediate vicinity of the body. It was impossible to secure the creek, but the officers made sure that the portion of the roadway that had become a part of the crime scene was contained.

"There must have been quite a fight," Johnson commented, after finding pools of blood, footprints, broken foliage, trampled mud, and blood splatters in various locations beyond the initially secured area. "Apparently, these persons had been running and fighting."

The tape was moved out to encompass the expanded crime scene each time new evidence was found. Again and again, the tape was relocated, finally surrounding a section of the campus that measured nearly sixty feet in width by one hundred feet in length. It was apparent to Johnson and Rector that the badly bludgeoned victim had put up an enormous struggle.

"What do we have here?" asked Detective Randy York, a twenty-five-year veteran of the Knoxville Police Department. York, assigned to the major crimes division of the KPD, had been instructed minutes earlier to report to the UT Agricultural campus. At 8:30 A.M., he arrived to find Officers Johnson and Rector cordoning off the quadrant.

"The body of a young white female," Johnson answered, guiding York to the brutally mutilated remains of the unknown female.

Detective York, dressed in a dark suit, shirt, and tie, his badge affixed to his left breast pocket, was immediately discernible from the uniformed officers. As lead detective, York took charge of the investigation. He ran his fingers through his black hair and shook his head. How could someone do this? Why? And most importantly, who?

Charley Belcher was sitting in the newsroom at WATE-TV in Knoxville. A former radio reporter, Belcher had just made the transition to television. It was his first day on the new job.

"Belcher, they just found a body on the UT campus. Get over there," the news director ordered him.

With cameraman in tow, Belcher raced to the crime scene. He was the first reporter to arrive.

Belcher, like the police cordoning off the scene, immediately thought the victim, a young white female according to officers, was a University of Tennessee student. The handsome young reporter stood in front of the police tape and presented the first shocking news of a body found on the UT campus. A body presumed to be that of a University of Tennessee coed.

Belcher's six-foot-two-inch frame shivered in the cold dampness of the early morning. His dark brown hair blew gently in the soft breeze as his hand tightly clutched the microphone. Belcher related as many details concerning the unidentified body as police had disclosed.

Speaking to Johnson, Rector, and York after his first broadcast, Belcher began to envision a crime scene more gruesome than he, or the police, had ever imagined. Over and over, officers described an incomprehensible display of human carnage.

York, along with other crime-scene investigators, thoroughly inspected the area for several hours. Clothing, hair, rocks, bones, and blood were systematically collected and preserved as evidence.

At 10:00 A.M., while officers from the University of Tennessee and Knoxville Police departments scoured the crime scene for evidence that would lead them to the killer or killers of the murdered girl, Christa Pike was in class at the Job Corps Center. Sitting next to her friend Stephanie Wilson at a small table, Christa smiled and nodded toward her feet. "That ain't mud on my shoes," she announced smugly. "That's blood."

Skeptical, Stephanie looked down at Christa's shoes. She could see dark spots under the light brown smudges of dried mud. But what did that prove? Christa loved to shock people.

"I have something to show you," Christa said. Grinning as though she was about to show Stephanie a treasured prize, she pulled a napkin out of her jacket pocket. Opening it slowly, she proudly said, "It's a piece of human skull."

Stephanie's brow wrinkled as she viewed the item curiously. "Whose?"

"Colleen Slemmer's," Christa said, satisfaction edging her words. "Tadaryl and I went walking with Colleen and I slashed her throat six times. I beat her in the head with a rock. Blood and brains were pouring out when I hit her in the head. Then I picked up a piece of her skull."

Stephanie stared at Christa in disbelief. Surely Christa couldn't be telling her the truth. Her statements were so matter-of-fact, so emotionless, Christa *must* be making it up.

"It wasn't planned. Just a spur-of-the moment thing. I just felt like it," Christa concluded.

Stephanie's conversation with Christa left her with unanswered questions. Why? Why would Christa kill Colleen Slemmer? And was it true, or a figment of Christa's vivid, tough-girl imagination? Christa showed no remorse, no regret, if indeed she had killed Colleen. She appeared as self-consumed and a braggart as always. If Christa had really killed Colleen, wouldn't she have to be mentally ill? As Stephanie's head filled with questions, Christa's attention returned to class.

At 3:15 P.M., Christa went to the office of Robert Pollock, orientation specialist for the Job Corps Center. She removed her black leather jacket, slipped it on the back of the first chair by the door, and sat down with Tadaryl Shipp next to her. Christa had lost her school ID. She was in Pollock's office to have a new one made. As soon as she had completed her mission, Christa and

A LOVE TO DIE FOR 47

Tadaryl left the building, inadvertently leaving the jacket and her grisly souvenir behind. At 4:05, when she returned to retrieve the forgotten garment, the doors were locked.

Christa Pike could no longer curb her curiosity. Had Colleen's body been discovered? What did the police know? Returning to the scene of the crime was the only way she'd find out.

"Will you go up to Tyson Park with me?" Christa asked another friend.

"Sure," Jennifer McCrary readily agreed. A few other students joined them.

With dark clouds and the threat of rain overhead, the gang of young people approached the park. Jennifer was surprised to see the area crowded with police. Police tape and uniformed officers kept them out of the area Christa had been headed for. The girls stood about fifty feet away from the secured section, watching as police collected evidence.

Officer Harold Underwood's assignment was to protect the crime scene, to make certain no one entered the area. He stood guard at one side of the yellow-and-black tape barrier.

"Why is this place taped off?" Christa asked Underwood, after moving in closer. The other girls remained back from the taped boundary.

"A body was found at this location," Underwood responded.

"Do you know who the victim is?" Christa asked.

"No," the officer responded, noticing the unusual pendant hanging from the girl's neck.

"Do you have any suspects? Any clues?" Christa persisted. Her dark eyes danced.

"We don't have a suspect and the victim is unidentified at this time," Underwood wearily responded. He watched the young girl with considerably more interest. Her behavior was uncharacteristic of most people who first learn of a murder. Instead of being shocked, scared, appalled, she appeared almost amused. Underwood's scrutiny deepened as she giggled and moved about with dancelike movements.

Christa was playing a game with Underwood. She already knew the answers to her questions.

Christa circled the area a number of times, trying to slip past officers, under the crime-scene tape, and into the area of investigation. Underwood kept a close eye on the girl, watching the teenager stare at the police, then at the crime scene, a grin on her face. It was if she knew a joke, one only she was privy to. By the time the gang of girls left, he was thoroughly disgusted by her macabre behavior.

Unable to obtain any further information or gain entry into the murder scene itself, Christa and her friends headed back up the strip toward the Job Corps campus.

"There's Tadaryl," Christa said, waving at the young man coming down the strip in the direction of Tyson Park.

"Why are you coming from there?" Tadaryl asked angrily. "We need to talk."

Jennifer and the other girls popped into the local Burger King for a Coke, leaving Tadaryl and Christa alone. Jennifer watched the two from the window of the restaurant. Although she couldn't hear their words, it was obvious to the young student that Christa and Tadaryl were arguing. Their voices were raised and the expression on Tadaryl's dark face indicated he was extremely irritated. *Just a lovers' quarrel,* Jennifer thought. Tadaryl and Christa had been dating for three or four months. Jennifer had never seen them fight. They wore matching pendants around their necks and were together constantly. They appeared to be well paired. If anything, Christa seemed obsessed with Tadaryl. She'd do anything for him.

Jennifer left the Burger King and made her way back across the street to Blockbuster, where she had seen Christa and Tadaryl disappear from view. There, in the store filled with videos and CDs, she found her friends listening to music on special headphones provided by the store. Whatever Christa and Tadaryl had been arguing about seemed to have vanished. The two were enjoying the music, smiling, and moving to the rhythms. There was no sign of conflict. No sign of distress. Christa and Tadaryl appeared perfectly content.

By late afternoon, two thousand safety alert fliers, warning UT students of the slaying on the UT grounds, had been posted around campus and at the married students' apartments. The fliers advised students to avoid walking alone at night, to not take shortcuts that might be unsafe, to report any suspicious people to police, to keep their doors locked, and to use the UT escort service.

The university, originally chartered as Blount College in 1794 and reorganized as the University of Tennessee in 1879, was ranked among the top fifty public universities in the country. The nationally ranked UT football team took the nickname "Volunteers" from the state's own byname honoring the thousands of Tennesseans who had volunteered and distinguished themselves in the War of 1812. The identity of the murder victim was still unknown, but speculation was high that she was one of the twenty-six thousand UT students enrolled on the Knoxville campus.

Police had described the victim as being eighteen to twenty-two-years old, five-feet, two-inches tall, and weighing one hundred and ten pounds. She had pierced ears and a mole on the left side of her stomach. She had light brown hair. She was wearing a pair of size-eight, white Nike Air sneakers, size-nine blue jeans with knots at the bottom of the pant legs, and a pink sweater with a blue design on the front. She could have been any one of the female students enrolled at the university.

Phillip Scheurer, UT Vice Chancellor for Student Affairs, was startled by the news of a death on his campus. "The university is as safe as the city of Knoxville is, and generally that's pretty safe," he told reporters. In the past, police had found non-students and homeless people near the bike trail, but they were trying to keep them out of the area. It was generally not a problem in cold weather, when the transients usually sought warm shelter. But the university was taking no chances. They posted warnings wherever the public might see them. They would take every precaution not to lose another student in a senseless slaying.

Four

In an attempt to identify the murdered girl, investigators scoured missing person reports at the Knoxville Police station, while crime-scene technicians combed the ground, brush, and trees behind the old steam plant for clues. Officer Lanny Janeway, along with KPD criminalists, began the tedious search.

Janeway ducked under the police barrier to get his first look at the murder scene. His attention was quickly drawn to a large pool of blood halfway up the road. Through the blood he could see drag marks and a small trail of the red liquid leading off to the right. Strands of light-colored hair were stuck to the edge of the road, held there by coagulated blood. Shoe prints were visible in a smaller pool of blood, with a second small puddle beside it.

Janeway's focus shifted to the victim sprawled in the briars and bushes. Her head tilted a little to the left; she was reclining on her left side, with both arms extended over her head.

"There's more blood down here," Sergeant

Brock called to Janeway. "The drippings lead past the service road to the bike trail."

Both men followed the path of blood drops and detected yet another small pool of blood. Their search was interrupted by the arrival of Dr. Gary Lethco, Knox County Medical Examiner. Together, the officers and ME approached the body. The policemen grimaced. "Gruesome" was the word Janeway would later use to describe the murder scene to reporter Charley Belcher.

The first, most obvious wound they observed, was a continuous cut across the back of the victim from the right shoulder to the left kidney. Several other slash marks also marred the victim's bare back.

Ambulance attendants reached the murder site and rolled the dead girl over for the medical examiner's initial visual inspection. A large gash at the throat and several smaller ones were partially obscured by a blood-soaked cloth around the throat. The jeans worn by the girl had been cut out in the crotch area. A large piece of blood-splattered asphalt lay at her feet.

Janeway continued his search of the area, finding the victim's bra eighty-three feet from the body, and an additional pool of blood twenty feet from the undergarment. Strands of hair were entwined in vines and tangled in leaves near the bra.

This was one hell of a struggle, Janeway thought as he gathered the evidence, stored each piece in a plastic bag, and instructed another officer on photographs needed for documentation. Their work would take several hours.

Detective York observed the Knoxville ambulance attendants as they placed the mutilated body of the girl in a black plastic body bag, laid her on a gurney, then loaded her in the ambulance for transport. Soon she would be en route to the medical examiner's office for an autopsy.

York watched as the ambulance pulled away, his dark eyes already weary. He planned to go to the morgue himself. Maybe the body could give them some indication of who the girl was—or who her killer might be.

Officer Cook of the University of Tennessee Police Department accompanied Dr. Lethco to the UT Autopsy and Forensic Pathology department to fingerprint the victim.

"I'll stay while you fume the body," Cook told Officer Crenshaw from KPD Criminalistics once he had completed the fingerprinting.

Crenshaw sheltered the portions of the body he planned to fume by constructing a tent made from plastic sheeting. Only those hairless regions of the body most likely to have been touched by the killer would be processed, such as the neck, face, and under areas of the arms.

Carefully Crenshaw squeezed droplets of super glue into a glass dish and placed it under the tent. He knew he had to work fast because once the glue was exposed to air, it quickly emitted vapors. He rapidly began fanning the fumes over the body. If any fingerprints were present, the gases would adhere to them, producing a milky-white color visible to the naked eye. As soon as prints appeared, Crenshaw hurriedly took photographs. He then dusted them with latent powder to turn the prints black, photographed them again, lifted them with tape, and placed them on cards. If any of the prints proved to be clear, they might be able to identify the killer.

Knox County Medical Examiner Dr. Sandra Elkins, who would perform the autopsy, had served as the director of Autopsy Services and Forensic Pathology at the University of Tennessee Medical Center since July 1994. In the six months since she had taken over the office, the board-certified physician had never encountered the type of human carnage on the postmortem table in front of her.

Dr. Elkins had unzipped the black body bag to find a corpse caked with mud, leaves, and twigs. A piece of fabric tied in a knot was slipped around the neck of the victim.

"There's a lot of work to do before I can evaluate the body," Dr. Elkins said with a sigh.

The young woman's body was lifted from the transport pouch and placed directly on the cold, stainless-steel table. Documentation photos of the body were taken from various angles. Then the remainder of her clothes—jeans, panties, shoes, and socks—was removed from the victim. The cloth, wet with blood and hair caught in the knot, was cut away from the victim's throat. A thin gold necklace was carefully extracted from the open gash in her neck. More photos were taken.

The arduous process of cleaning the body began. Dr. Elkins meticulously picked twigs and grass from the mud-encrusted portions of the torso. Gently, she washed the blood and dirt from the cadaver, exposing the extensive number of scrapes, cuts, and slashes that covered the entire torso of the unidentified victim.

Dr. Elkins took a deep breath. Her job had only begun. From the introductory observation, she could see that documenting each injury of this victim would take a great deal of time. The medical examiner immediately decided to save the head for last. That was where the most extensive injuries were located.

"I'm going to start on the torso and upper extremities," Dr. Elkins said, speaking into a recorder. "I'll try to document the major sharp force or slash and stab wounds first."

With the victim facedown on the examining table, Dr. Elkins began identifying each wound, labeling it with a letter, and photographing it for documentation.

"The first cut is a linear slash wound, or a superficial wound made with a sharp object," she reported. "It is four-and-one-quarter inches in length and is located on the victim's upper back." Dr. Elkins labeled the wound with the letter "A."

" 'B' is also a slash wound. It is to the right side of the back and measures three-and-one-half inches in length. 'C,' another slash wound, runs diagonally across the back. 'C' measures eight-and-a-half inches in length. 'D' is also a slash wound, running diagonally across the back four inches."

Dr. Elkins stopped to take a deep breath. She had just begun the autopsy procedure, but knew from the wound-riddled body she would be there for some time.

" 'E' is a stab wound to the back, a little over a third of an inch in length and three-quarters of an inch in depth. Slash wound 'F' is to the right arm, just above the elbow. It is four-point-eight inches in length. 'G' is a slash wound to the right lower arm and measures point-thirty-four inches in length. 'H' is another slash wound to the right arm. It is one-half inch long. 'I' is also a slash wound to the right arm and measures one-point-seven inches in length. I'd call these defense wounds," Dr. Elkins stated. The victim had instinctively tried to use her arms to shield off the weapon coming at her.

Dr. Elkins studied the area around each wound. All showed a vital reaction, a red appearance, indicating that the heart was still beating and the blood vessels in the skin were reacting to the injury. The victim was alive when each of the wounds was inflicted.

Dr. Elkins carefully rolled the corpse over on her back and continued the examination.

" 'J' is a stab wound to the lower left side of the abdomen and is approximately eight-tenths of an inch in depth. 'K' is a long slash wound to the front of the chest that goes longitudinally from the chest, between the breasts all the way down to the abdomen and ends right about where the navel is. It measures eleven-and-a-half inches in length." This slash was the longest, most prominent injury visible on the victim's chest.

" 'L,' another slash wound to the front of the chest and abdominal area, measures seven-point-two inches," Dr. Elkins stated. The shorter slash mark, "L," ran vertically parallel to wound "K." In contrast, slash wound "M" ran horizontally across the upper abdomen.

"Slash wound 'N' is to the upper abdominal region, going across the upper abdomen and measures five-point-five inches in length. 'O' is also a slash wound running basically diagonally across the upper abdomen, measuring five inches in length, and 'P,' also running horizontally, measures four-and-a-half inches in length. 'Q' is another slash running horizontally across the abdomen, just above the navel and is three inches in length."

Dr. Elkins paused. The victim had been marked with two vertical slashes and a number of horizontal ones. The killer didn't go for the quick kill. These were not life-threatening wounds, but torturous carvings. The victim had been alive, watching the destruction of her own body, undoubtedly in horror.

The medical examiner began again. " 'R' runs across the lower back, and measures three-and-one-half inches in length. 'S' is a gaping incised wound. It crosses the middle of the neck and measures six inches in length."

Most of the wounds documented by Dr. Elkins to this point had been slash wounds, generally superficial. The gaping incised wound across the victim's neck was deeper. It had gone through the fat and muscles of the front of the neck making it possible for Dr. Elkins to see the muscles of the neck without having to stretch it apart.

" 'T' is a slash that crosses the bridge of the nose, the left side of the face, and under the eye. It measures two-point-nine inches in length."

Up to this point in the autopsy, Dr. Elkins had described slashes or stabs made with a sharp instrument, but when the medical examiner reached the wound she labeled "U," the structure of the wound was different. "U" was a laceration caused by actual tearing of the skin by a blunt object that hits the skin with enough force to exceed the elasticity of the skin so that it tears.

" 'U' is a laceration," Dr. Elkins stated. "It is above the right eye, in the eyebrow region. At its greatest dimension, it measures two-point-thirty-seven inches. It is a rugged tear. 'V' is also a laceration. It is to the right forehead and measures one-point-sixty-five inches in its greatest dimension."

Dr. Elkins suspended the procedure momentarily before proceeding to wound "W." She carefully studied the markings on the victim's chest. There was a pattern: a five-pointed star.

Continuing with the autopsy, wound "W" referred to a large area on the left side of the victim's head. It was a large tissue defect that basically ran from the left eye toward the back of the left side of the head, and curved around the left ear, or what was left of it. The ear was very mangled and hanging down. Dr. Elkins knew she was dealing with more than one laceration, but since it was all connected, she assigned it the letter "W."

Again, Dr. Elkins noted that the victim was still alive when wounds "U," "V," and "W" were inflicted, as determined from the red scraping or abrasions around the wounds. Not only was the victim alive, but more than likely she'd been conscious. "U," "V," and "W" caused breaking or fracturing of the skull, but Dr. Elkins noted that blood had begun to fill the sinus region of the victim, indicating she was still alive after the three massive blows to the head. Then she'd aspirated that blood into her airway and down into the lungs.

The last wound labeled by the Knox County Medical Examiner was "X," a slash wound to the left side of the face that ran under the left ear and measured two-point-eight inches in length. There were numerous other wounds on the body. Some of these wounds were abrasions and contusions. The abrasions were like those often found when a child falls and scrapes its knee. The contusions were bruises where there is bleeding in tissue and fat under the skin. Each of the bruises on the victim was purple in color, indicating a fresh wound.

Contusions were found on the knees of the victim—wounds consistent with crawling on the ground or on asphalt. And the abrasions on the breast were consistent with someone being dragged by her feet while her chest scraped the ground.

In addition, the doctor found bruising of the inner part of the upper lip, as well as multiple small lacerations inside the lower lip, consistent with some kind of overlying object forced on the lips up against the teeth, causing the bruising and tearing. Abrasions also appeared on the chin.

It was obvious to Dr. Elkins that she would be forced to start the alphabet over in order to list each wound individually. The procedure could take days. Dr. Elkins threw her hands in the air and made one final declaration: "Innumerable more superficial slash wounds on the back, arms, and chest."

Officer Cook returned to the morgue, accompanied by a woman. She had called the PD concerning her missing sister, mentioning that she had a small mole in the abdominal area. Cook knew their Jane Doe had just such a marking.

The woman timidly walked to the table and stared at the dead girl. She expelled the breath she had been holding and told Cook, "It's not her."

Detective York arrived and stood across from

Dr. Elkins at the examining table. "What do we have?" York asked.

Dr. Elkins quickly ran through each of the wounds she had recorded for her report. Then she pointed out the configuration on the chest area of the victim.

"Looks like a five-pointed star. A pentagram," York remarked. Then he made a mental note to have investigators check to see if any reports of satanic activity had come in to the station.

Prior to performing the final procedure, the removal of the head from the body, Dr. Elkins carefully sawed the skull cap from the head and extracted the entire brain. "There are multiple loose pieces of skull that were driven into the left side of the brain," Dr. Elkins explained. "And black firm particles within the soft tissue."

Painstakingly, Dr. Elkins removed as many of the pieces as possible. Each and every fragment that was in the brain was not retrievable, but the doctor collected a number of small shards that had broken loose. The head was then amputated from the body and the soft tissue, mainly skin, and a slight amount of fat and muscle, was removed, revealing the skeletal structure of the skull. Dr. Elkins was able to determine that a number of blows to the head had occurred, and had ultimately caused the death of the young woman. In order to be certain of the number of blows sustained by the victim, as well as how the wounds had been inflicted, the skull was prepared to be forwarded to the office of Dr. Murray

Marks, assistant professor of Anthropology at the University of Tennessee, for further evaluation.

Except for consulting with Dr. Marks on the number of blows sustained to the head, Dr. Elkins's autopsy was complete. Her initial conclusion was that the victim had been alive and conscious during the entire time her body was being beaten and cut. The blows to the head had probably caused her death.

The skull of the victim would be an essential piece of evidence if the case ever went to trial. In a bizarre move, the skin of the victim, containing what was believed to be a pentagram design, as well as her genitals, were also preserved for possible evidentiary value. Elkins's reasoning was that it was best to retain any feasible piece of evidence in order to help explain to a jury the viciousness of the attack, and how the injuries had occurred.

Detective York still had no idea who his Jane Doe victim could be, but he knew she had suffered a horrendous death. The pentagram cut in her chest might give them a lead to her identity. He returned to the police department, instructed detectives to be on the lookout for any type of satanic activity, and then he headed home. It had been a long day. A frustrating day. One dead body. No real clues. Maybe tomorrow he'd get a break.

Five

The intrusive ring of the phone shattered Detective Randy York's tranquil sleep. As he reached for the receiver, his gaze fell on the luminous face of the clock on his bedside table. It was 2:30 A.M. York picked up the phone.

"Yeah, York," he said sleepily.

"Detective, some lady called the station a few minutes ago. She was real upset," the dispatcher told York. "Said her daughter called her and told her a bunch of kids at the Job Corps are involved in satanism. She said a girl had been murdered and her daughter's terrified."

York hung up the receiver and lay back down. He tossed and turned, trying to avoid the voice inside him that kept saying to get up and check out the story. No information about satanic evidence, in conjunction with their murdered Jane Doe, had been released to the press. This could be a break. Finally, he gave in to his intuition and got out of bed.

"Where are you going?" York's wife asked.

A LOVE TO DIE FOR   65

"I've got to go in. I've got to check out that call," York said, buttoning his shirt.

The seasoned detective was familiar with the Knoxville Job Corps. Numerous complaints had been leveled by various business owners, particularly those along the strip. Charges of shoplifting, vandalism, and disorderly conduct plagued the Job Corps program.

Originally established by the Economic Opportunity Act of 1964, under the administration of the Department of Labor, the Job Corps was created as an effort to help hard-core, unemployable youth. Students were generally high school dropouts. Many were from broken homes, surviving on public assistance.

The program, a part of President Lyndon B. Johnson's War on Poverty, was designed to break the cycle of poverty and to give students individual vocational, educational, and social skills training to prepare them for permanent employment. But the success of the Knoxville program was questionable.

For the more than one hundred centers across the county, with about sixty-three-thousand students, the question had become whether the Job Corps was a training program or a quasi-correctional program. The Knoxville center had become one of those with serious management and disciplinary problems.

A lack of adequate supervision had set loose on the community a number of disruptive youths, many of whom had already had brushes with the law. Business owners in Knoxville were fed up with the incidents that besieged their establishments. Complaints against the Job Corps had become a thorn in the side of the Knoxville Police Department.

At 4:30 A.M. York arrived at the Job Corps campus and found the female student's room on the second floor of the dormitory. Nervous and quivering as she spoke to York, she agreed to accompany him downtown to the Knoxville Police Department.

In a trembling voice, the young black girl related a story of satanic worship and murder.

"Tell me the names of all the people that were involved," York instructed her.

"Christa Pike, Tadaryl Shipp, and Shadolla Peterson," the girl responded. "Christa and Tadaryl bragged about the killing. They're getting ready to leave town."

York left the informant with the pledge that the three would be picked up immediately and she needn't worry. But York's assurances did little to alleviate her sense of doom. She planned to leave Knoxville for home as soon as possible.

York drove straight back to the Job Corps campus. He first reviewed the checkout sheet posted with security and found that four students had checked out on Thursday, January 12, but only three had returned to campus. The fourth was still missing. Colleen Slemmer.

At 5:30 A.M. York was knocking on the door of Christa Pike.

A LOVE TO DIE FOR   67

A childlike girl answered the door. Her round face and large dark eyes made her look younger than her years. She looked sweet and vulnerable, not cold and callous, as York had imagined.

"I need you to come to the police department with me," York told Christa. "I need to ask you some questions."

Christa, Tadaryl, and Shadolla were taken to the main room of the Knoxville Police Department. Quickly, York escorted Christa to a separate interview room, where they could speak in private.

The mild-mannered York chatted with the suspect for a few minutes before questioning her about the murder. His handsome smile and soft brown eyes seemed to relax Christa, setting her at ease.

"Is that a tattoo?" York asked, noticing a small figure visible on Christa's chest.

"Yes, it's a little devil," Christa said in a childlike manner. She pulled her top down slightly, exposing a full view of the tattoo. Under the small figure were the words, "Litl Devil."

"Christa, I need to give you a Miranda warning," York said. Then he read Christa her rights under the law and allowed her to read the warning before she signed it.

"Would you like to give us a statement concerning the girl whose body was found on the UT Ag campus?" York asked.

"Yeah, under certain conditions. If I don't have to mention who else was with me," Christa bargained.

York agreed, pushed the button on the tabletop tape recorder, and Christa began making her statement.

"The girl was Colleen Slemmer," Christa began.

The eighteen-year-old told York that she and Colleen had been having problems for a long time.

"She'd run her mouth and be up in my face," Christa said. The childlike manner was quickly disappearing.

Christa explained how she had asked Colleen to go to Blockbuster, then tricked her into going to Tyson Park on the pretense of smoking marijuana.

"I told her I had a bag of weed up in Tyson Park. She could come up there and we'd get all high and everything," Christa stated with a smile.

Then Christa began an animated, descriptive narration of the night of terror for Colleen Slemmer.

"I thought I was going crazy 'cause I'd never seen myself act like that before in my life," Christa explained. "I've never been so mad in my life. I guess I didn't know when to stop, but I just kept hitting her. I threw her on the ground and started kicking her and kicking her and kicking her. I picked up her head and hit her head into the concrete, but it never hurt her."

Christa appeared to want York to know every detail of what she seemed to think of as a great adventure.

"I told her to shut up and I just kicked her in the face. I kept kicking her. I don't know where all the kicks landed. I just kept kicking her. I know I kicked her in the face and then in the side and I don't know where all else. She just kept laying there crying. She tried to get up and run and the other person that was with me caught up with her and pushed her down to the ground. He pushed her down on the ground and she just lay there. She was trying to get back up—like crawling. We were holding her. We dragged her," Christa said.

As Christa continued her oral statement, she told York about cutting Colleen on the stomach with the box cutter. Then she heard someone yelling for her to do something, because Colleen would tell on her and that she would go to jail.

"Then I started thinking, that's true. If she gets up from here, I'm good as gone. You know? She's already cut. You know? That would be attempted murder. Another person had cut her chest. He didn't cut her on the stomach. He cut her on the chest," Christa continued in a matter-of-fact manner.

Next, Christa described cutting Colleen's back as she attempted to run, then pushing her into the bushes. Colleen had begged Christa to listen. Begged Christa to stop.

"I said, 'Quiet. Shut up! I don't want to hear

you talking to me.' It's harder to hurt somebody when they're talking to you," Christa said, almost laughingly.

York looked at the teen inquisitively. The girl he'd thought sweet looking at first sight was now proving herself to be as lethal a killer as any he'd ever encountered.

Christa went on to describe how Colleen kept saying she would leave and not tell anybody what had happened. "She wouldn't shut up," Christa said. "She just kept talking, and talking and kept talking. I kicked her in the face and I'd say, 'Shut up!' She would start talking again. I didn't want to hear her talking."

Christa told York that, although Colleen continued to talk to her, she could no longer hear the words.

"I didn't know what happened. Like I floated out of my body and it wasn't me anymore. I was just watching everything that was happening. It sounds stupid, but it's not. I was just watching. I could see me standing there," Christa said.

With little emotion and no sign of remorse, Christa told York the details of the beating, slashing, and ultimate death of Colleen Slemmer. York sat spellbound by the intense, literal account of the killing. Most adult offenders he had encountered had not spoken with such clarity and description. The young teenager who sat across from him was an enigma. How had she arrived at the point of accepting death, and more importantly, killing, as a seemingly normal occurrence?

York's thoughts were interrupted as Christa continued her confession.

"I was like, I gotta go. We walked down and washed our hands in a mud puddle that was at the bottom of the hill. I washed my shoes off a little bit. Then we went back. We stopped at this gas station and I washed my hands and everything off to where it looked halfway decent," Christa confessed.

"What about your clothes?" York asked.

"There's a pair of jeans turned inside out on top of my suitcase that have blood on them. And the shoes. You do all the tests. I have blood in my shoe strings. I don't care anymore," Christa told York. "They're on top of my suitcase in my bedroom."

"What about the box cutter?" York questioned her.

"We threw it. I don't remember where. I cut her back with a thing that looked like a little mini meat cleaver or something," Christa said, seemingly tired from the ordeal.

"Did the other person use that to cut her?" York inquired.

"I don't know what he used to cut her."

"What did you do with her? Just leave her laying there?"

"I picked up one of her legs by her ankle and the other person picked up her other leg, and we drug her off to the side of the road and laid her aside, up the hill. On a pile of dirt. There was some trees. She was there by her sweater and some other things. The bra was still on her arm, I'm pretty sure. It may not have been," Christa said, somewhat unclear on that subject.

"Do you know what the design cut in Colleen's chest was?" York asked.

"No, I cut her one time on her chest and the other person cut her on the chest. I just sliced her. I don't know. I don't know if the other person cut something in her chest. I was just screaming at her," Christa replied.

"Is Tadaryl Shipp involved in satanism?" York asked.

"I don't know. I know he wears a pentagram around his neck just like I have a pentagram around my neck. But it was just a Christmas present from a friend. He has never tried to get me involved in anything like satanism. I don't know if he's involved. He doesn't talk about it."

"Do you dabble in satanism?"

"No, no, I believe in God, you know," Christa answered. "I'm not— There's no way. I'm just interested. Tadaryl doesn't talk to me about it. I know he used to have a satanic bible he was reading one day. That's the only thing I know he's ever done."

York asked what had been done to Colleen's jeans. Christa explained the cut marks near the crotch, stating that she had just intended to scare Colleen. Then Christa began talking about her feelings for Tadaryl.

"I love him to death. I mean I really do, and I don't want to see anything happen to him. I

A LOVE TO DIE FOR

don't care if I am by myself, you know. I don't want to see nothing happen to him. He's strong minded most of the time. He's been going through a lot lately, and he's even been crying to me, like real tears out of his eyes. Crying before any of this even happened. We've both been real stressed out. I don't want to see anything happen to him because he has the potential to be something, to be somebody. I don't feel I have—just because of everything I've tried and done. I've always fucked it up somehow. I don't want him to end up being like I am," Christa said, her concern for Tadaryl undeniable.

"You've been pretty candid about what happened, Christa. Has it been bothering you?" York asked.

"Yeah, a lot."

York doubted that statement. Christa had shown no remorse for her actions. She'd told the story of the horrendous death of Colleen Slemmer as though she was telling him about a trip to Disney World. The experienced police officer could not think of another suspect he had interviewed in his eighteen years as a detective with the lack of conscience that Christa Pike showed.

Christa finished her statement by telling York that she had thrown a pair of black gloves and two identification cards belonging to Colleen in the trash can at the Texaco station on the strip. The mini meat cleaver she had returned to the person she'd borrowed it from at the dorm.

Christa's statement was complete.

York took a deep breath. The events Christa Pike described to him fit the physical evidence at the scene, as well as the wounds found on the victim's body.

He knew without a doubt that he had the killer.

Six

Christa read and signed a written transcription of her confession, along with a consent to search her dormitory room. She was then escorted to a holding room.

Impatiently, York had to wait nearly five hours before questioning Tadaryl Shipp. Official permission had to be obtained in order to speak with the seventeen-year-old, who under the law was considered a juvenile.

Finally, York and Tadaryl were face-to-face. Although quite a bit shorter and stockier than York, Tadaryl looked older than his seventeen years. His thick dark eyebrows were highly arched, setting off steel-cold eyes that burned a hole in you like fire through paper.

York made a mental note of the pentagram medallion, hanging from a metal chain, that Tadaryl wore around his neck. Christa Pike wore an identical medallion. Tadaryl also wore a blue-colored crystal mounted in a double-hand setting and a hand-or-claw shaped bauble, both on a black cord. Dangling from his ear was a hexagram earring. Pinned to his ball cap was a hexagram pin. York ordered photographs taken of both youths wearing the satanic-themed jewelry.

As with Christa, York read Tadaryl his Miranda Rights, then had him read and sign them. York again pushed the button on the police department tape recorder, and began questioning Tadaryl.

Shipp seemed likable. He spoke calmly, with no emotion in his voice. Like Christa, Tadaryl was candid about the killing of Colleen Slemmer. He talked about taking Colleen to Tyson Park, Christa beating her, the pentagram he cut in her chest, and the death blows to her head. York had never seen a murder more monstrous, nor a suspect with a more lackadaisical attitude than Tadaryl Shipp.

"I walked away when Christa began hitting her in the head with asphalt chunks," Tadaryl said, after admitting he had tripped Colleen when she tried to run away.

"She just laid there gasping and breathing," Tadaryl stated calmly. No emotion was in his voice. No remorse was in his eyes.

Tadaryl confessed to returning to help Christa dump the body on a pile of refuse. Cutting the pentagram in Colleen's chest was an idea that "just came in my mind," Tadaryl told York.

Showing no restraint, Tadaryl explained his interest in the satanic, and that he had been worshipping the devil since he was eleven years old. "After the murder, I thought about it being a sacrifice," Tadaryl said. He admitted feeling that the act was related to paying homage to the devil.

York ran his fingers through his thick, dark hair. He was beginning to see the evil that lurked in the mind of this young teen. Tadaryl's nickname, "Baby Satan," seemed apropos.

Tadaryl stated that the clothes he had worn on the night of the killing were still in his room at the Job Corps Center. He signed a consent to search which read:

> *I, Tadaryl Shipp, having been informed of my constitutional right not to have a search made of the premises hereinafter mentioned without a search warrant and of my right to refuse to consent to such a search, hereby authorize Mark Waggoner and Lanny Janeway, Officers of the Knoxville, Tennessee Police Department, to conduct a complete search of my premises located at [ ] Dale Ave., Job Corps Center, Room [ ].*
>
> *These officers are authorized by me to take from my premises any letters, papers, materials or other property which they may desire.*
>
> *This written permission is being given by me to the above named officers voluntarily and without threats or promises of any kind.*

The document was signed by Tadaryl Shipp and witnessed by Randy York on January 14, 1995.

Tadaryl was transferred to a holding room, separate from Christa Pike's. Although fatigued and incensed by Christa and Tadaryl's accounts of the murder, York proceeded to interview the last of the three suspects, Shadolla Peterson.

Shadolla's dark eyes looked tired. She admitted that she knew that Christa Pike had intended to confront Colleen Slemmer in Tyson Park on the night of the murder, but denied any knowledge of a preplanned killing. She described in exacting detail the events of the evening, the acts of Christa and Tadaryl, and her instructions from them to keep quiet. She rejected any suggestion that she had participated in the murder of Colleen Slemmer.

Within thirty-six hours of the killing, Pike, Shipp, and Peterson were arrested. York knew he had the killers. All that was left was to gather the evidence needed to ensure their convictions.

"I want you to go to the suspects' rooms at the Job Corps and gather any evidence you find," York instructed Officer Lanny Janeway.

Officer Mark Waggoner was dispatched to the Texaco station, where Christa claimed to have deposited Colleen's identification cards and a pair of gloves. York requested dental records of Colleen Slemmer for a positive ID on the victim. The case was falling together quicker than York had ever expected.

Janeway arrived at Shipp's dormitory room on the Job Corps campus about 2:45 P.M. A security guard from the Job Corps Center and Tadaryl's roommate were waiting for the officer.

"Which lockers are Tadaryl Shipp's?" Janeway asked the young student.

"Over there," said the teenager, pointing to the lockers belonging to his roommate.

Janeway, an experienced evidence technician, removed a pair of black nylon jogging pants, two black T-shirts, and a black, hooded sweatshirt from a dresser drawer. In addition to the clothing, Janeway secured a satanic bible from the same dresser. He turned the book over, inspecting it closely. A pentagram adorned the front cover.

A shiver went down Janeway's spine as he recognized the symbol as similar to the one he had seen on the chest of the murder victim.

The officer bagged the evidence, along with an arm cast, tennis shoes, a meat cleaver, and a box cutter found in Tadaryl's room. After marking the evidence for identification, Janeway moved on to Christa Pike's room.

Folded neatly on top of a suitcase at the top of her closet was a pair of Guess blue jeans, just as Christa had described to York. The jeans had a black leather belt, with silver buckle and tip, drawn through the belt loops. Dark, brownish-colored spots were visible through dried dirt on the bottom portion of each jeans leg. Several cuts were visible in the heavy fabric. Janeway carefully folded the garment and placed it in an evidence bag.

As Janeway surveyed the room for other items pertinent to the case, he took a small satanic statue from the dresser top. The silver-colored image was of a figure with ram horns twisting to each side of the head. The horns began in the middle of the forehead from a red-colored stone. In his hands was a sword. At his feet, a clear crystal rested on a hexagram affixed to the base.

All of the clothing collected from the suspects' rooms, along with Christa's Fila tennis shoes and Tadaryl's Nike tennis shoes, would be sent to the Tennessee Bureau of Investigation in Nashville for blood analysis.

Meanwhile, Officer Mark Waggoner went to the Favorite Mart/Texaco station on Cumberland Avenue near Tyson Park. The eight-year veteran of the criminalistics unit of the Knoxville Police Department found a pair of ladies' black gloves near the bottom of the women's room trash can. Inside the gloves were three identification cards.

One card was a Florida driver's license, stamped "ID only." The card bore the name and photo of Colleen Slemmer, along with other identifying information.

The second card was just an ordinary ID, and the third a Job Corps ID. Waggoner looked at the photo of Slemmer momentarily. The attractive, smiling girl in the picture bore no resemblance to the mutilated face belonging to the victim found near Tyson Park. Waggoner slipped the items in an evidence bag, sealed it, and proceeded to the station's Dumpster outside the building. Finding nothing of evidentiary value on his initial inspection, Waggoner called the FBI to pick up the container for further scrutiny. Then he returned to the police station.

A LOVE TO DIE FOR

* * *

When Janeway arrived back at the PD from the Job Corps Center, York instructed him to get a video camera and follow him to Tyson Park. York was taking Christa back to the scene of the crime.

Sitting beside York in the Knoxville Police vehicle, Christa directed the detective to the remote area of the University of Tennessee campus where Colleen had been killed. Retracing her steps, she guided York down Seventeenth Street to a side street off the main drag, then out to the strip on Cumberland Avenue, and on to Tyson Park. York and Christa exited the car at the picnic area by Third Creek.

Christa shivered from the cold, creek-chilled wind that blew across the picnic area.

With Janeway following behind them, Christa and York crossed the Third Creek bridge, went through the short tunnel, and down the bike trail beside an open soccer field. York slowed his pace to match Christa's. Her stride was no match for that of the tall police detective.

Christa was bubbly and chatty as they walked along the trail. She seemed to take pleasure in relating every detail of how she had lured Colleen to the area. When the trio arrived at the murder scene, Christa became remarkably animated. She told York how she first hit Colleen in the face with her fist, swinging her arm wildly in the air.

"She fell down," Christa said, falling to the ground herself.

"She put her hands over her face like this," she stated, while she demonstrated Colleen's actions.

Then, before York could grasp what the young girl was doing, she was up, swinging wildly again. Christa was acting out the murder. Portraying her part as the murderer and Colleen's as the victim. York stood and watched in amazement.

Christa made slashing motions in the air as she described slicing Colleen with the box cutter. She again fell to the ground and clawed at the earth, just as Colleen Slemmer had done in her attempt to get away from her attacker.

"I told her to shut up and I kicked her in the face. I just kept kicking her," Christa said, as she kicked at an imaginary victim. "I was just looking at her and watching her bleed."

Then Christa lay back down on the ground. "She rolled over and she got up and tried to run again. I cut her on the back," Christa told them. The suspect rolled in the dirt, got up, then arched her back as if in pain, mocking her victim.

York noticed a smirk on the face of the young killer. She seemed to be enjoying the reenactment—perhaps as much as she had enjoyed the kill. The detective shot a quick glance at Janeway. He wanted to make certain the officer was getting all this on tape.

Christa lifted her arms over her head, and

thrust them downward as though striking Colleen on the head with the asphalt chunk.

"I could hear her breathing. She was like breathing blood in and out. Kind of gurgling. And she was just jumping like this, jerking," Christa said, making her body duplicate the twitching movements made by the dying victim.

Then she leaned over, as if speaking to Colleen. "I said, 'Colleen, do you know what's doing this to you?'"

The video ran as Christa danced around in a circle singing, "La, la, la, la, la."

York was stunned. Christa Pike was having a good time. She looked at Janeway and smiled. It was as though she was a star giving an award-winning performance. Christa Pike was playing to the camera.

York was prepared to make his charge. He had statements from the three suspects, evidence collected from their rooms, a video reenactment of the crime, and confirmation on the identity of the victim. There was only one thing left to do. Arrest the suspects.

January 14, 1995, two days after the murder of Colleen Slemmer, Christa Pike of Durham, North Carolina, Tadaryl Shipp of Memphis, Tennessee, and Shadolla Peterson of Cleveland, Tennessee, were arrested, each charged with first-degree murder. The front-page headline of *The Knoxville News-Sentinel* seemed to ease the minds of frightened residents: 3 TEENS CHARGED IN SLAYING; JOB

CORPS ROMANTIC TRIANGLE CITED IN TORTURE KILLING."

Police Chief Phil Keith stood at the police station podium, dressed smartly in a suit, white shirt, and tie, and stated for reporters that the arrests should squash speculation that the murder was the result of a kidnapping involving a university student. Keith pledged to step up patrols on the bike path, just to lessen any further worries of residents.

But as the fears of the people of Knoxville diminished, a mother's worst horror was just beginning.

May Martinez arrived at the Knoxville airport and was met by Detective Randy York. The handsome policeman tried his best to give May a warm greeting, but his duty was a hard one, even for the seasoned officer.

"I don't know how to tell you this, but your daughter was brutally mutilated and murdered," York finally said.

"Okay." May's simple answer was low, remote, unbelieving. She couldn't accept what York was telling her. Colleen wasn't dead. This was just a terrible mistake.

York drove May to the office of Dr. Sandra Elkins, Knox County Medical Examiner. There, May was shown photographs of her daughter's bloody, mangled body. She stared at the photos questioningly. That wasn't Colleen. There was no resemblance between her lovely daughter and the battered form she saw sprawled in the brush. The head, the body, they were not Colleen's. Again, she thought, there must be some mistake.

Randy York took May to the police station and informed her of the suspects in custody and the statements they had given concerning the murder. The sympathetic detective promised to keep her informed of any developments in the case.

May made the short drive across town from the police station to the Job Corps Center. Although Colleen had told her of the condition of the dorm, May was horrified to see the purple ceilings, graffiti on the walls, and unsupervised teens running up and down the halls screaming. She realized why Colleen had been so unhappy there.

When May asked for Colleen's personal belongings, she was told that her room had been ransacked and most of her things stolen. May was handed three pairs of socks—all that were left of Colleen's personal effects. Despondent, May returned to Florida. To Colleen's empty room. But she still didn't believe that Colleen was dead.

Two weeks later, Knox County General Sessions Court Judge Geoff Emery denied Christa Pike the option of keeping her original one-hundred-thousand-dollar bond and ordered she be held without bond. William Crabtree of the Knox County District Attorney's Office was pleased with the judge's decision. Known as a tough, hard-nosed prosecutor, Crabtree had already announced his intention to seek the death penalty in the Pike case.

Christa didn't seem to mind being in jail. She appeared to actually enjoy the notoriety.

At the encouragement of fellow inmates, the youthful murder suspect would get on the floor of the jail and play out the murder for her new admirers. She assumed the role of victim and killer, just as she had done in front of York and Janeway and the video camera.

"I'm as happy as I've ever been," Christa told a relative from the jailhouse phone. "I can't go down the jail row without having to sign autographs. I'm famous."

Seven

As the news of the Job Corps murder broke on Saturday, January 14, 1995, word spread through Knoxville like a fire through the Great Smoky Mountains. Town talk concentrated on the three Job Corps students arrested for murder and their nineteen-year-old victim. More attention than ever was focused on the Job Corps program.

Charley Belcher hadn't covered any extraordinary events on the downtown Corps campus while reporting for local Knoxville radio. A few fights had been it. Now, with news of the murder, stories of thefts, assaults, and disorderly conduct were running rampant throughout the city. He decided to pull the crime statistics and judge how viable the rumors were.

Belcher found that the crime stats for the University of Tennessee students were much higher than those reported cases of Job Corps related crime. When Belcher asked the Knoxville Police Department for comment, he was told, yes, the instances of crime by UT students was higher, but that he had to take into consideration that the rate was spread out over twenty-six-thousand students. Accounts of Job Corps student-related crime were concentrated on only three hundred and fifty persons.

Belcher didn't buy it. He believed the Knoxville Police were frustrated with the Corps kids and would embrace any reason to take action in seeing that the program was shut down.

Belcher had to admit that interest in the Job Corps had risen greatly, and in particular, interest in the four students involved in murder.

Detective York began an investigation into the backgrounds of each of the suspects, as well as the victim. None of the four students had any criminal record, either as juveniles or adults. Only Christa had had any brush with the law, and she hadn't been charged with any crime. The lack of legal trouble left York wondering: what brought the students to the Knoxville Job Corps, and what had happened to facilitate murder?

Colleen Slemmer

Colleen Slemmer had dropped out of high school, worked fast-food jobs, and was headed for a life of low-paying, menial employment when she first learned about the Job Corps. By signing the contract committing to the full length of the computer-training program, Colleen seized the opportunity to better her life.

But like most students who end up in the government-sponsored program, Colleen took with her to Knoxville a hardened attitude and some definite ideas about how she would live her life.

May Martinez confirmed to Randy York that Colleen had been practicing white witchcraft. Colleen was one of many Americans who had joined a revival of witchcraft in the second half of the twentieth century. A continuation of the practices of the native religions and cultural beliefs of Europe after the advent of Christianity, white witchcraft was a name given to the pagan worshipers by the Christian Church. Especially popular in contemporary professional communities, the New Age focus had moved away from accepting God as a male figure to recognizing male and female duality, as found in nature.

Under the umbrella of Paganism, nature or earth-oriented religions, White Witchcraft is heavily based in tradition. Unlike Satanism, White Witchcraft has nothing to do with either the philosophy or anti-Christian religion of Satanism. Witchcraft teaches that you should follow your heart and take responsibility for your own actions. The magical tradition teaches, "The whole of the action is the sum of its consequences." White witches follow the philosophy of "live and let live." White witchcraft, unlike black magic or black witchcraft, is used for good, not evil.

White witches are not born, but made by becoming a practitioner of the religion. A form of self-dedication, a conscious decision to follow the Old Ways, must be made to the Gods and Goddesses. All the basic beliefs of the religion must be followed: keeping of secrets or mysteries of the religion; an initiation that may include family traditions, after reaching a specific time in life, a measured time of study, or performing specific tasks; the God and Goddess are aspects of nature who do not reign over the Universe, but are the Universe; and the Other World is where Ancestors dwell and the two worlds meet at places like trees, hills, lakes, rivers, caverns, and areas where thick mists dwell.

Steeped in ritual, tools of White Witchcraft include the Sacred Blade, used by witches to move and direct energy in a focused manner and for bloodletting. The Chalice is the symbolic womb of the Goddess and is associated with fertility. To drink from the Chalice is to drink of life. The Cauldron is used to make things that are imbedded with magical properties. The Wand is used to move energy over a wide or dispersed area. It is also used as a test of chastity. The ringing of the Bell marks time and purifies the air of unwanted influences. It calls the spirits and is used to create an altered state of consciousness.

White witches look down on Satanism, believing that evil will come back threefold to those who engage in evil actions and in harming others. Colleen Slemmer's religious beliefs, her opinions of life itself, were in direct opposition to those of Tadaryl Shipp.

During his interview with Detective York, Tadaryl had informed the officer that he believed

Colleen was a witch. The youth had no doubt that the only way to kill a witch was by crushing her skull. Satanists also believe that a body has to be whole for its soul to escape. With Christa keeping the piece of Colleen's skull, perhaps Tadaryl believed they would be keeping her soul captive.

Christa Pike

Born to Carissa and Glenn Pike, Christa's struggle in life came quickly, beginning with a premature birth. The sick infant, with huge brown eyes and dark hair, was taken from her mother's arms and rushed to a nearby hospital for special neonatal care. The four-day separation of mother and child negated any initial bonding, and any maternal attachment with Christa would have to wait even longer. With Glenn Pike out of work, Carissa was forced to keep two jobs in an effort to feed her family.

Christa was a typical toddler, her dark pigtails swinging to the music as she twirled around the floor in her pink tights, tutu, and ballet slippers. Her bright eyes danced as her feet kept beat to the music. But Christa's happiness was short lived.

Carissa Pike divorced Glenn, leaving two-year-old Christa to be cared for by her grandmothers while her mother continued to work two jobs. In her rare free time, Carissa chose to date rather than spend time with Christa. Zola Fotos, Carissa's mother, was a verbally abusive alcoholic who beat Christa and put her in a closet for long periods at a time. At an early age, Christa learned to hate Grandma Fotos.

When Carissa was home with Christa, the child was most often uncared for. Carrie Ross, Carissa's sister, would drop by to find a filthy house with a sink full of dirty dishes and little Christa crawling through dog poop. Ross often took Christa and her sister, Alicia, to her house to eat. She frequently bought them clothes. At Ross's house Christa could be a kid. Play dress-up. Have dolls.

Christa then began living with Delfa Pike, her paternal grandmother, when Carissa decided to take off with one of her boyfriends and move to North Carolina. Although her mother deserted her, Delfa loved Christa, and nurtured her. They read books. Cooked. Played. The aging grandmother and fragile granddaughter were inseparable. Delfa Pike gave her granddaughter something she had not had since birth: a sense of belonging.

At age eight, Christa's world came crashing down. Grandma Delfa was dead. Cancer had taken hold of her body, eaten away her spirit. Christa was devastated. She had begged to stay home from school to nurse her grandmother back to health. She wanted to be the same kind of caregiver Grandma Pike had been to her. No one would allow it. When Delfa Pike died, Christa felt she had failed her.

As Delfa Pike lay cold in her coffin, Christa's short legs took her to the front of the church to see her beloved grandmother. Seeing Delfa's wax-like image lifeless in the satin-lined box, Christa could no longer contain her grief. The small child became hysterical. Sobbing. Yelling out in pain for the one person in the world she knew loved her. At age eight, Christa's world ceased to exist. Bitterness seemed to consume the child. She became a problem for everyone, including family, teachers, friends. Christa's anger over the abandonment of her grandmother could not be controlled. She did not know how to express her grief, her fears. At age eight, Christa Pike overdosed.

At the suggestion of school authorities, Carissa took Christa to a psychiatrist. The initial session was the only visit Christa made. Perhaps Christa rebelled against any future therapy. Perhaps Carissa couldn't be bothered with making sure Christa kept her appointments. Whatever the reason, Christa failed to get the help she desperately needed.

With Christa's behavior reeling further out of control, Carissa decided to send her to live with Glenn. But her father could not harness the hostility that raged within her any more than his ex-wife could. Christa behaved badly and performed poorly in school. Glenn sent her back to Carissa.

Christa made the journey between the houses of her mother and father several times. Each time one of her parents found her behavior too difficult to deal with, she was sent away, engendering a feeling of being rejected by each parent repeatedly.

By the time Christa was thirteen, Glenn had

remarried and begun a new family. Christa was jealous of the attention her father gave his wife and newest baby daughter. When the two-year-old toddler showed signs of sexual abuse, Glenn sent Christa packing for the last time.

The alienation from her father only sent Christa further over the edge into a world of depression and destruction. She refused to go to school. She threatened her mother's boyfriend with a knife. She roamed the streets at all hours. She smoked pot. She had a live-in boyfriend. Her actions screamed for help. But instead of taking control and giving Christa the guidance she needed, Carissa decided to become her daughter's friend. They drank together, and smoked dope together.

Not until Christa and a friend kicked in the door of someone's house did Carissa decide that Christa had been given enough chances in life. It was time for Christa to grow up. Time for her to get her act together. No more second chances. Christa would join the Job Corps.

In the late summer of 1994, about the same time Colleen Slemmer was leaving her Orange Park, Florida, home headed for Knoxville, Christa Pike was saying good-bye to family and friends in Durham, North Carolina. The Job Corps was her last chance to straighten out her rebellious life.

Christa watched the lights of Durham fade in the distance as the bus rolled along Interstate 40 toward Knoxville. She knew if she hadn't messed up she would be home in Durham, rather than headed toward a strange new city.

Durham, always known for its fine smoking tobacco, Bull Durham the most notable, would be forever remembered for the baseball term "bullpen." The term was coined because of a Bull Durham tobacco ad painted behind the dugout of the New York Yankees. The prosperous textile materials industry, including denim, hosiery, and colored yarns, had declined, with medicine and technology taking center stage in the late 1950s. With eleven colleges and universities in the Durham area, Christa Pike had ample opportunity to better herself. But Christa wasn't interested in education. It was fun and good times she sought and she found them almost immediately at the Job Corps Center. They came in the shape of Tadaryl Shipp.

The young white girl from North Carolina took an instant liking to the short, muscular African American. She claimed him as her own and defied anyone to come between them. He was her lover. Her best friend. She would keep him at all costs.

The defiant teen, determined to play out her tough-girl role, began taunting Colleen Slemmer within weeks of checking into the job training center. Whether real or imagined, Christa saw the taller, leaner, older girl as a threat to her happiness. She couldn't, she wouldn't, let Colleen come between her and Tadaryl.

Tadaryl Shipp

Tadaryl Shipp called Memphis home. Although he had spent the first years of his life in Mississippi, Tadaryl moved to Memphis, Tennessee, at age nine to live with his mother and stepfather. The move had been unsettling for young Tadaryl. His grades fell from A's to B's and C's.

Tadaryl's mother, Emery Charlton, became concerned about her son. His behavior changed. His grades continued to plummet. She feared a school gang was after him to join their ranks. But Tadaryl hadn't joined a gang, he had become involved in Satanism.

Like most adolescents who become interested in satanic worship, Tadaryl may have been looking for control over his life, or simply a way to rebel. According to Terry Moyers, a police officer who teaches police officers about the occult, the "nontraditional youth subculture" of satanism believe they can cast spells, raise demons, and anything they do is all right, as long as it is in the name of Satan. These young worshipers of Satan don't kill to gain power, but to draw energy out of their victims through attacking them. The crime scenes are commonly bloody, because the immense amounts of blood get "the flow going of the energy source."

Satanic worshipers follow Satan's philosophy that you get what you can and do what you want to do. The practice is egotistical, selfish, and self-centered. For followers it is a way to make their lives more exciting, especially when blood is involved or the sacrifice of animals.

Life isn't sacred to the satanist. The giving up of a life is accepted. The taking of a life condoned.

A LOVE TO DIE FOR 97

Tadaryl advocated the modification of the Golden Rule, as set down by Satan: "Do unto others as they do unto you." There is no evil. No guilt. One acts on natural instinct. Followers of Satan do not pray to God for assistance or forgiveness because they believe Satan has the power.

Emery Charlton had conferred with the school principal, school administrators, with anyone who might help her guide Tadaryl in the right direction. She considered withdrawing him from his Memphis school and enrolling him in an Alabama military school, but the school was expensive. Even with Emery's salary as a payroll administrator for Coca-Cola and her husband's position as area manager for Nike, the financial burden of military school was too great for them to bear.

At age sixteen, Tadaryl Shipp packed up and headed for Knoxville and the Job Corps. With the promise of eventually attending the University of Tennessee, Tadaryl left behind the familiar sounds of the blues that poured from the open club doors on Beal Street, the hordes of tourists that visited Graceland, illustrious home of Elvis Presley, and the delicious taste of Memphis barbecue.

Tadaryl took with him his acceptance of Satan and the belief in the nine statements as written in the Satanic Bible.

1. Indulgence instead of abstinence.
2. Existence instead of spiritual pipe dreams.
3. Undefiled wisdom instead of critical self-deceit.

4. Kindness to those who deserve it instead of love wasted on ingrates.
5. Revenge instead of turning the other cheek.
6. Responsibility to the responsible instead of concern for psychic vampires.
7. Satan represents man as just another animal who, of divine spiritual and intelligent development, has become the most vicious animal of all.
8. Satan represents all the so-called sins because they lead to mental or emotional gratification.
9. Satan is the best friend the church has ever had because he has kept the church in business all these years.

Tadaryl hadn't been on campus long when he met Christa Pike, a cute, bubbly, white girl from North Carolina with an infectious smile and adorable Southern accent. They became instantly connected—mentally and sexually. The couple was inseparable. Christa fed his male ego, he introduced her to the teachings of Satan. It was a pairing made in hell. The early development of a gruesome twosome.

Shadolla Peterson

The least known of the four Job Corps students who captured the front page of *The Knoxville News-Sentinel* was Shadolla Peterson. Even after a preliminary background check, Detective York didn't know much about the third suspect in the murder of Colleen Slemmer.

Shadolla was a quiet girl with dark skin and sad

brown eyes. She grew up poor in Cleveland, Tennessee, right in the heart of the Smoky Mountains. Shadolla had left the lush forests, winding rivers, and Southern hospitality of Cleveland to seek her future at the Knoxville Job Corps. An education that would help her to climb out of a legacy of poverty.

Shadolla had no idea when she befriended Christa Pike that her life would be forever changed.

Detective York, as well as reporters Charley Belcher and John North, would continue to seek information on the lives of Slemmer, Pike, Shipp, and Peterson. York worked to prepare an ironclad case to ensure convictions; Belcher and North struggled to help answer the question that remained for most of their viewers and readers.

Why?

Eight

The headline of *The Knoxville News-Sentinel* shocked Robert Pollock: 3 TEENS CHARGED IN SLAYING. The photos of Colleen Slemmer, Christa Pike, Shadolla Peterson, and Tadaryl Shipp glared at him from the front page. He had interacted with all four students at the Job Corps Center.

As Orientation Specialist, Pollock knew all of the students. Colleen had been a favorite of his. Her easygoing personality and infectious smile had made her a popular student. She'd frequented his office, and he'd felt like a substitute father to the homesick youth.

Pollock was devastated to learn that Colleen was dead.

On Tuesday, January 17, 1995, after a three-day holiday to celebrate the birthday of Martin Luther King, Pollock returned to his office. As soon as he opened the door, he noticed a black leather jacket hanging on the back of a chair.

Someone must have left it here on Friday, Pollock thought, as he reached for the coat. He picked it up and looked it over. He would describe the garment as an "Elvis Presley"–looking jacket—early Elvis, in his opinion. Then he remembered who had been sitting in that chair just before closing on Friday, the thirteenth. Christa Pike.

Without delay Pollock called Captain Hudson of Job Corps security, reporting he was in possession of Christa Pike's jacket. Then, carefully held by two fingers, he took the item of clothing to Hudson's office.

Hudson patted down the pockets of the short, black jacket to see if anything was concealed within them. He felt an object. Leaving the unidentified article safely in the pocket, Hudson telephoned the Knoxville Police Department.

"A black coat thought to have been worn by Christa Pike has been recovered at the Job Corps," the radio dispatcher told Arthur Bohanan, Knoxville Police crime specialist. "Can you go down and examine the coat and pick it up?"

Bohanan, a twenty-two-year police veteran, confirmed that he was on his way to the Job Corps campus. At 8:10 A.M. Bohanan was standing in Hudson's security office.

The police specialist carefully reached into the left pocket of the coat. He found a plastic fork—and a piece of bone.

Bohanan took the bone to Dr. Murray Marks at the University of Tennessee anthropology department, and the coat to the police station.

* * *

Satanism and murder added to the list of concerns business persons and citizens of Knoxville had with the Job Corps Center. There was a rumbling within the community to oust the center from their peaceful town.

A police investigation of alleged occult activity at the Job Corps was conducted to find out how prevalent satanic worship was on campus, and just how many students were involved. During the investigation, it was discovered that Tadaryl Shipp had created an altar, for satanic worship, complete with statue, in his dorm room. The altar, a sacred place, was erected to put Tadaryl in the spiritual mood.

"There may be a small group, five to fifteen students who dabble in the occult, but are not seriously involved," a report issued by the police department said. "It docs not appear that there is an organized group at the Job Corps Center or that any type of Satanic worship occurs on the center grounds. Based on our investigation, we believe that Shipp and Pike were the persons most deeply involved in the occult."

Investigators did discover, however, that a local woman identifying herself as a Wiccan priestess had visited the Job Corps and distributed occult-oriented comic books and drawings of animal claws holding objects.

Although the Job Corps had beefed up patrols, adding four security officers to its staff, and directed staff members to undergo a week of training on the occult and how to recognize items associated with alternative religion, the people of Knoxville were not satisfied. They wanted the Job Corps banned from their city. Local police were also ready to see them go.

In 1994, forty students from the Knoxville Job Corps program were charged with crimes ranging from misdemeanors, such as curfew violations, to felonies, such as rape, robbery, and assault. The number of offenders had tripled in two years.

In November 1995, Knoxville Police Chief Phil Keith announced that a seven-week study revealed a nearly four-hundred-percent increase in police calls prompted by the Job Corps Center. The report, compiled by the Knoxville Police Department, reflected interviews conducted with residents and business leaders.

"I'm going to send copies to both senators and all nine congressmen, as well as the Secretary of Housing and Urban Development," Keith said.

Keith believed his report would be of special interest on Capitol Hill, where one billion dollars had been allocated for the national program. Twenty-three-thousand dollars per student was set aside for training, with a dropout rate of thirty-seven percent in the first ninety days, and only about thirteen percent of students finding jobs immediately in the area for which they were trained. Overall about seventy percent were placed in some kind of job or in another school.

There were success stories. The most prominent Job Corps alumni was heavyweight boxing champion George Foreman. Foreman was taken from the mean streets of his California neighborhood and a nightmare lifestyle to the achievement of his most incredible dreams. Foreman credits his Job Corps experience for helping him reach his goals.

But the few success stories were offset by stories of fights, frequent drug use, and students engaging in sexual activity within the dorms.

Chief Keith had written letters to Job Corps managers outlining problems with its students and security measures, but nothing had been done. More than once, officers armed with arrest warrants for students were told the students were unavailable, even though they were on campus. Records showed Job Corps officials had picked up students at the juvenile detention center charged with crimes, then allowed them to leave the state before their court dates. Keith charged the Job Corps with an "irresponsible attitude."

Seven months prior to the release of the Knoxville Police study, prompted by the outcries of concerned citizens, the three hundred and fifty student Job Corps Center, a converted inner-city motel on Dale Avenue, was closed, ending its fifteen-year residency in Knoxville.

The murder of Colleen Slemmer had become known as the "Job Corps Murder." The murder destroyed not only human lives, but the center itself. Yielding to the demands of the community, the government closed it within three months of Colleen Slemmer's death.

The report by Chief Keith had confirmed the

feeling of outraged citizens; crime around the center declined by more than twenty-two percent within the first six months after the center closed its doors.

"The impact was very significant, not only in crime, but in general disorder," Keith said.

Charley Belcher still questioned the crime statistics indicating large numbers of incidents on or near the campus, but the people of Knoxville were delighted to see the Job Corps leave town. Only two blemishes left by the Job Corps' presence remained: the trials of Christa Pike and Tadaryl Shipp.

Nine

Tadaryl Shipp stood calmly in the hallway of the Knoxville City-County Building waiting to enter the courtroom. The January 16 hearing had been called to determine if Tadaryl, who was being held at Knox County Juvenile Detention Facility, would continue to be treated as a juvenile, or if he would stand trial for the murder of Colleen Slemmer as an adult.

Tadaryl was quiet. His dark eyes showed the strain of the three days he had spent in detention.

When the hearing began, it was the Knox County prosecutors who took center stage. They presented explosive evidence that supported their contentions that Tadaryl should be tried for his crime as an adult, and thus be eligible for the death penalty or the minimum of life imprisonment.

An eerie silence fell over the courtroom when William Crabtree, lead prosecutor for the case, played the tape-recorded words of Tadaryl on the morning of his confession.

"She just laid there gasping and breathing," the defendant said with no emotion.

Charley Belcher gasped audibly. He had been the first reporter on the scene. He'd known immediately that the murder of the Job Corps coed would be a big story, but after hearing the chilling words of Tadaryl Shipp, Belcher was convinced that the Job Corps murder was going to be a huge story. He frantically took notes for his later broadcast.

To add further impact to Shipp's words, a Knoxville police officer described how the young defendant had fallen asleep on the floor of the police station after confessing. "He showed absolutely no remorse whatsoever," the officer told the court. Tadaryl appeared to wear the same regretless expression in court.

But the court wasn't swayed by the impact of the youth's confession. The judge ruled that the seventeen-year-old would continue to be treated as a juvenile. Tadaryl Shipp, unlike his girlfriend, Christa, had dodged the threat of the death penalty.

The following week, Christa Pike and Shadolla Peterson were in court for bond hearings. Although dressed in identical Knox County Jail jumpsuits, the similarity between the two girls stopped there. Shadolla was solemn, almost withdrawn, while Christa smiled, scanning the courtroom to see who had come to see her in court. She grinned broadly at Charley Belcher sitting in the gallery.

Bonds for both girls were initially set at one hundred thousand dollars, more than Christa's family could raise. However, Shadolla was able to post bond almost immediately and was released into the care of her family in Cleveland, Tennessee.

A short time later, Shadolla exited the Knox County Jail with a bag of clothes slung over her back. She remained quiet, ignoring requests for comments from the local press. Unlike Christa, Shadolla shunned the publicity, avoiding the increasing notoriety.

Assistant District Attorney Jo Helm seized the opportunity during the hearing to approach the bench and ask that Christa Pike's bond be revoked. The skilled female prosecutor stressed to Judge Geoff Emery that Christa's crime was a capital offense, and thus warranted confinement to ensure her appearance in court. Over the adamant protests of defense attorney William Brown, who argued that Christa was not a devil worshiper and that she had no hand in carving the pentagram on Colleen Slemmer's chest, Judge Emery denied bond. Christa would spend the next fourteen months in the Knox County Jail awaiting trial. Christa gave no indication that she minded the prospect of spending the next year in the Knoxville jail. She had made friends, been given attention. In less than two weeks, Christa Pike had become a celebrity, both inside and outside of jail.

* * *

Three weeks after being released on bond, Shadolla Peterson was back in court. This time to appear at a probable cause hearing. Looking rested and well groomed, Shadolla's posture was slumped, her sad brown eyes cast downward.

Shadolla admitted to being at the scene of the crime, but denied having anything to do with the murder itself. Knoxville Police disagreed. "We know she was there and we believe she took part in it," said Foster Arnett, spokesman for the police department.

But the police had no physical evidence to link Shadolla to Colleen's slaying. No bloody clothing. No confession. Although the first-degree-murder charge was dropped, Shadolla would still have to stand trial for the charge of accessory to murder.

With trial dates set for all three defendants, prosecutors and defense attorneys alike began their tedious preparations. District Attorneys Crabtree and Helm were determined to win three convictions. They would begin with the capital murder case of Christa Pike. A death-penalty conviction would send a message not only to the other defendants in the Colleen Slemmer case, but to anyone who might commit murder in the city by the river.

Christa Pike would go on trial in March 1996.

Ten

March 25, 1996, May and Raul Martinez sat in the front row of Knox County Courtroom Number Three. They were the same seats they had occupied during the five days of jury selection for the first-degree-murder trial of Christa Pike—their daughter's killer. The bleak courtroom was void of decoration, except for one picture, the Tennessee state flag, and the American flag. An eagle emblem hung above where Judge Leibowitz would take her seat. The jury box was to the Martinezes's left, the prosecutor's table directly in front of them. The defense table, where Christa would sit, was across the aisle, a podium separating the prosecutors from the defense. The witness stand was closest to the jury box, with the court clerk at the opposite end of the judge's bench.

Over two hundred and forty potential jurors had been called. Fifteen people had been selected, twelve jurors and three alternates. The selection was a laborious task. Many of the potential jurors were uncertain they could invoke the death penalty. Others had heard at least something about the gruesome case, prompting defense attorney William Talman to request a change of venue.

"Your Honor, frankly, once you've heard the information in this case, you can't unhear it," Talman told Judge Leibowitz.

But Leibowitz had been convinced that a jury could be seated and denied the petition.

May's long blond hair was neatly pulled back in a ponytail, fastened by a decorative hair ornament. Bangs softened her forehead. May's attractive features closely resembled those of Colleen's.

May gripped the edge of the hard wooden bench tightly. She had waited fourteen months to see her daughter's killer brought to trial. Finally, the day had come. It was difficult being in Knoxville; there was the memory of Colleen, the leaving of her youngest daughter back in Florida, and the expenses. The costs were mounting—motel, food, travel, but she and Raul had to be there. For Colleen. For themselves.

May stiffened as the side door swung open and Christa Pike emerged from the secured hall adjacent to the courtroom. Christa had been led from the jail in the basement of the County-City Building through a maze of corridors and private elevators. The ritual would be repeated several times each day during the course of the trial.

The ex-Job Corps student looked pale. Christa hadn't been outside her jail cell, except for court hearings, in over a year.

May studied Christa closely. The wild look of a rebellious teenager was gone. Her hair was smoothly pulled back from her face and neatly secured with a white ribbon. Her face was freshly scrubbed. Christa's dress, trimmed with a white lace collar, presented the image of a young schoolgirl rather than a defiant dropout accused of one of the most heinous crimes in Knoxville history.

Christa Pike's courtroom make-over infuriated May. She wanted the judge and jury to see Christa for what she was—a cold-blooded killer—not the young ingenue her defense attorneys were attempting to portray.

May's anger escalated within moments of Christa entering the courtroom. Christa was smiling, almost giggling, and waving to her mother. Tears of pain swelled in May's eyes. Her daughter wasn't there to wave to her. She clenched her fists and took a long, deep breath. Judge Mary Beth Leibowitz was taking her place on the bench and the long-awaited trial was about to begin.

Judge Leibowitz was a no-frills person. The only jewelry she wore was a plain gold wedding band. Her chin-length, brown hair was worn in natural waves. Leibowitz's round face wore a nice smile, but under the pleasant exterior was an authoritative, strong-willed woman. A woman capable of controlling the high-profile, emotionally volatile proceedings expected in the Christa Pike trial.

Assistant District Attorneys William Crabtree and Jo Helm straightened the pads and pens on the prosecutor's table. They were well prepared for the murder trial of Christa Pike. Crabtree was the longest serving assistant district attorney in Knox County, having been with the office since 1976. He was regarded as an authority on Tennessee law. Helm, a former newspaper reporter, had joined the DA's office ten years earlier. They had worked together on several cases, but none as disturbing as the Pike case.

Christa was young, but one of the most merciless killers Crabtree and Helm had ever encountered. For that reason, Crabtree, the lead prosecutor, was seeking the death penalty. If found guilty, Christa would be the youngest woman on death row in the United States.

Crabtree glanced at May and Raul Martinez, sitting in the gallery. He nodded slightly, then rose to give his opening statement.

"We are here today about the tragic death of Colleen Slemmer. We are here today about the business of murder," Crabtree began solemnly.

"The testimony of the witnesses that you are going to hear, the exhibits that you are going to see, the evidence that is going to be introduced to you are going to show you an act that is so vile, so heinous, so atrocious, so despicable . . . as bad or worse than anything you've ever seen in a movie, read in a novel, or experienced in your worst nightmare."

May fought back the tears. She was about to relive her own personal nightmare, as well as her daughter's.

Crabtree ran down a list of witnesses he expected to call, then added, "And from the testimony of these witnesses, the proof is going to show you that, on the twelfth day of January 1995, Colleen Slemmer was a living person, a student at the Job Corps."

The assistant district attorney stood before the jury as he presented his statement. An imposing figure at more than six feet tall, the silver-haired Crabtree knew that winning his case began here, with his opening remarks. He adjusted his metal-rimmed glasses before continuing.

"Colleen Slemmer went to Tyson Park with this defendant and a couple of friends, Tadaryl Shipp and Shadolla Peterson. While she was there, these people, led by this defendant," Crabtree said, while pointing to Christa sitting at the defense table, "used a knife to slash her entire body. They used pieces of asphalt to crush her skull. And then when they got through doing these things to her, they dragged her body to a pile of asphalt and dumped it there."

May Martinez stared at the jury, looking for any reaction, any indication they understood the torment her daughter had been forced to endure.

"The next morning," Crabtree continued, "Mr. Sutherland comes along and sees this body, nude from the waist up, completely covered with blood. The head completely distorted from what these individuals had done to her.

"Law enforcement agents come. They do an investigation at the scene. Talking about blood and parts of the victim's clothing found over sixty, seventy, eighty feet from the body.

"And Dr. Elkins is going to tell you how she does her reports. That she uses letters to indicate the injuries when she examines a body for the purposes of autopsy. That when she did the physical examination on Colleen Slemmer, she went all the way to 'X.' Twenty-four separate injuries that she identified.

"She will also tell you that if she had identified the minor ones, she could have gone through the alphabet two or three more times. This is the degree of injuries that we are talking about being inflicted on Colleen Slemmer."

Christa Pike's expression was woeful as Crabtree described Colleen Slemmer's wounds. She began to weep softly, then rested her head on the defense table.

"Dr. Elkins is going to tell you that there are ten slash wounds to her throat. That her throat was actually cut ten separate times. She is going to tell you about and show you the pentagram that was carved on her chest. She is going to tell you about and show you the slashes that run all the way across her back, and the stab wounds on her back. And the fact that her head was beat to the extent that it actually split her skull in two."

As Crabtree elaborated on the victim's injuries, Christa stared down teary eyed at the defense table, the picture of remorse.

"And Dr. Elkins is going to tell you that, except for the injuries to the head, the beating that completely broke the skull in two, that Colleen Slemmer was alive when all these other injuries were inflicted on her.

"And she was alive when this person was slicing her throat ten times!" Crabtree's voice rose to an excited level as he pointed another accusing finger at Christa Pike.

"And she died because of these injuries that were inflicted by the defendant and her friends." Crabtree paused momentarily to take a long breath.

"And then you are going to hear a statement of this defendant, a recorded statement, that she gave to the police department. And in her own statement, she tells you that Colleen Slemmer was alive while they are cutting her and while they were carving a pentagram on her chest. And in that statement she tells how Colleen would jump up and try to run and she would throw something and hit Colleen in the head and knock her down. And how they were cutting her throat and she wouldn't die. She was laying there moaning and groaning and she would not die! She'll tell you then about picking up a piece of asphalt and bashing her head in," Crabtree said, as some members of the jury shifted uncomfortably in their seats.

"And then, the last vile despicable act that the state is going to show you that this person did, is she reaches down into this bloody mass of Colleen Slemmer's head and she takes a piece of skull as a souvenir.

"That's the business we are here about. Very serious business." Crabtree's voice lowered. He walked to the defense table and stared at Christa Pike.

"And we are going to show you that the person seated over here is not some twenty-year-old little girl everyone is looking at. This is a vile, despicable human being who has committed a vile, despicable act. The act of murder in the first degree."

Crabtree walked to the prosecution table and sat down. His words had captured the attention of the jury and spectators alike. Crabtree's opening remarks were the first sign of the gut-wrenching, horrendous testimony that the State planned to present.

Though sick at heart over what she'd heard, May Martinez was pleased with Crabtree's opening. He had managed to point out that under the sweet exterior of Christa Pike beat the heart of a devil. Across the courtroom, the mood was different. Tears tumbled down the cheeks of Christa's mom, Carissa Hansen. She had sympathy for May Martinez, but Carissa Hansen didn't want to lose her daughter, too.

Julie Martin, co-counsel for the defense, stood and approached the jury. Her long, light-brown hair was pulled back from her face and secured with a large bow. Spectators wondered what defense Talman and Martin would take with a defendant who had confessed to such a shocking crime.

"The state may or may not be able to prove some of the essential elements of the offense charged, murder in the first degree," Martin began. "Those essential elements are: one, that Ms. Pike unlawfully killed the alleged victim; two, that Ms. Pike acted intentionally. Three, the killing was deliberate. A deliberate act is one performed with cool purpose. And four, that the killing was premeditated. A premeditated act is one done after the exercise of reflection and judgment.

"It is not necessary that the purpose to kill preexists in the mind of the accused for any period of time. It is sufficient that it preceded the act, however short the interval, as long as it is the result of reflection and judgment," the young attorney explained.

"The mental state of the accused at the time that she allegedly decided to kill must be carefully considered in order to determine whether the accused was sufficiently free from the excitement and passion as to be capable of premeditation.

"Furthermore, premeditation can be found if the decision to kill is first formed during the heat of passion, but the accused commits the act after the passion has subsided," Martin informed the jury.

It was clear to judge, prosecutors, spectators, and reporters the defense would be working to keep Christa off death row by challenging her mental state at the time of the murder. They wanted the jury to believe the murder had not been premeditated.

To May Martinez, it didn't matter when Christa Pike had decided to kill her daughter. Colleen was dead. She hoped this jury would be willing to take the life of the person who'd killed her.

"Some of the evidence that you will see in here may be gruesome, may be graphic, may be absolutely horrible. But remember, you must set aside your emotions and decide this case only on the facts and the evidence. And you must find that the state has proven each and every essential element beyond a reasonable doubt before you may convict of first-degree murder," Martin concluded.

The well-intended defense attorney's opening statement had lasted only three minutes. With an oral confession, forensic evidence, and eyewitness testimony working against their client, Martin and Talman had their work cut out for them.

Carissa Hansen looked at her daughter lovingly. She didn't see the killer the prosecutors, and even Christa's own defense attorney had just described. Carissa saw someone else. She saw a tiny, three-year-old ballerina in pink tights and tutu, dancing on her tiptoes. She saw the smile of an angel, not the heart of a devil.

Petite, dark-haired Judge Leibowitz peered over her glasses and looked down from her raised bench at Assistant District Attorney William Crabtree.

"Are you ready to begin the prosecution, General?" Judge Leibowitz asked, shortening his official title of "Assistant District Attorney General."

"The state's ready, Your Honor."

Officer John Johnson, the first University of Tennessee police officer to reach Colleen Slemmer's body, gave the first indication that the trial of Christa Pike would be difficult for jurors and spectators to bear.

"The head had been completely bludgeoned," Officer Johnson responded to a question from Assistant District Attorney Bill Crabtree. "It was just a bloody mass of hair and blood."

"Could you see the face?" Crabtree inquired.

"I believe that's what I was looking at. It was so mutilated," Johnson replied.

At the end of Johnson's testimony, Judge Leibowitz announced, "Due to the lateness of the hour, we'll adjourn.

"Ladies and gentlemen, due to all of the coughing, sneezing, and hacking in the courtroom, please drink lots of orange juice over the evening and morning and get a good night's rest. I need all of you all the way through this, and I thank you very much for your time and your patience with all of us today, and for the last few days. We have a few days to go together.

"Please go with the officers. Have a good evening and a good dinner. Relax. And we'll see you tomorrow morning."

Eleven

The defacement of the victim implied by Officer Johnson the first day of testimony, was strikingly brought to light when Medical Examiner Dr. Sandra Elkins took the stand the following morning. From the beginning of her testimony, everyone who filled the small courtroom was besieged by the description of the violent killing of Colleen Slemmer. As Elkins identified more than fifteen individual slash wounds, one nearly a foot long, stab wounds to the back and abdomen, scrapes on the face, and a gaping cut across the throat of the victim, the defendant and May Martinez wept.

Christa dabbed her eyes with a white tissue handed her by defense counsel Julie Martin. May stared at Christa, resentment tightening her eyes. She wondered where the tears were when her daughter was begging for her life.

Elkins detailed each of the wounds, as requested by Assistant District Attorney Crabtree. She proceeded through her lettering system, stopping at one point to clarify the difference between the types of wounds.

"Both a slash and a stab are made by a sharp instrument," Dr. Elkins explained. "However, a slash wound is longer than it is deep in contrast to a stab wound, that is deeper than it is long. A slash wound is more of a motion like that." The doctor made a sweeping movement with her arm. "A stab wound is more like this." She thrust her arm downward.

"Can you say whether the victim was alive at the time these wounds you've described so far were inflicted?" Crabtree asked.

"All of these wounds were inflicted while the victim was still alive. If a wound is inflicted while the heart is still beating, the wound has somewhat of a red appearance. That's because the blood vessels in the skin are reacting to the injury.

"A wound inflicted after death, when a heart has quit pumping and there is no blood pressure, has no bleeding, no tissue reaction to the injury, because the person is no longer pumping blood. There is no pressure to get the blood out to the injured area. So when a wound is inflicted after death, it has a very bland, parchmentlike color, just a yellow or brown color," Elkins explained.

As Dr. Elkins described Colleen's appearance, May visualized the photos the doctor had shown her when she first arrived in Knoxville after Colleen's death. She hadn't believed it was her daughter. Wouldn't let herself believe it was Colleen.

Elkins told the jurors that none of the wounds

described so far would have caused the victim to lose consciousness.

"Doctor, concerning these slash wounds that you have testified to on the neck and around the eyes, and I believe on the nose, can you tell us whether or not the same instrument was used to cause those that was used to cause the lacerations that you labeled on the head 'U' and 'V'? Are we talking about two different kinds of instruments being used?"

"Two different types of force," the doctor responded.

"Okay. And the slash wounds are caused by what type of instrument?" Crabtree asked.

"A sharp object."

"And the lacerations?" Crabtree probed.

"They were caused by a blunt object."

"So it appears that two types of weapons were used to the face of this individual, is that correct?" Crabtree attempted to clarify.

"Yes," Dr. Elkins said, making it clear that Colleen Slemmer had been cut on the face with one type of instrument and hit on the head with another. Wounds "U," "V," and "W" were lacerations, tearing the tissue by blunt force.

"Is that where the massive damage was done?" Crabtree asked.

"Yes."

"Now at the time that 'U,' 'V,' and 'W' were inflicted, was the victim alive?" Crabtree questioned.

"Yes. The scraping or abrasions around the wounds on the head were red," Elkins answered.

The forensic pathologist went on to explain that not only was the victim alive but that, again, none of the injuries that had been inflicted upon her body would have caused her to have lost consciousness.

May clenched her teeth and tightly closed her eyes. Colleen had been alive throughout the entire ordeal. She had felt every sting of the cutter and cleaver, every impact of the asphalt. What was going through Colleen's mind as they were cutting her? May wondered. As she attempted to shake the image of her daughter lying bloodied and beaten in the mud on the deserted University of Tennessee roadway, Crabtree approached the bench.

"I think it was requested that we approach the court before we attempt to introduce the skull," Crabtree said, addressing Judge Leibowitz.

The judge requested that the jury leave the courtroom before arguments were held on the admission of the skull as evidence.

"Let the record reflect that Dr. Elkins asked for a glass of water and I just gave her a glass of the best jail tea you can ever imagine," Leibowitz announced.

Spectators, which included some University of Tennessee students, and attorneys from both sides smiled at the lighthearted comment by Leibowitz. The experienced, well-liked judge knew how to put a courtroom at ease.

Leibowitz was framed by a navy blue wall, flanked on her right by the American flag and on her left by the state flag of Tennessee. The judge was a Knoxville native, a graduate of William and Mary, and Dayton School of Law. Originally appointed to the bench, she had successfully run unopposed in her last two elections. Known for her common sense, as well as her knowledge of the law, Leibowitz was proud to be noted as the judge with the fewest reversals in the state. She intended for this trial to go as smoothly as previous litigations.

After the jury retired to the jury room, Leibowitz returned to the serious question of evidence to be introduced by the state.

"General, you had indicated while you were at the bench that there had been some motions regarding some evidence, and they include the skull and the skull fragments. And you are going to be hauling them out right now," Leibowitz said to Crabtree.

May Martinez went cold. She stared at the judge in horror. What did she mean, haul out the skull and skull fragments? Colleen's skull? May had not been allowed to view Colleen's body. She had been told by authorities that it would be better if she did not see the mutilation of her daughter firsthand. The photos she had seen showed her daughter's battered body, complete with skull. It had been newspaperman John North who had informed her that Colleen's skull had been removed. If the state successfully entered the head of her daughter into evidence, it would be the first time May would see the bare skull of her dead daughter. May felt as though she were in someone else's body, someone else's mind. This could not be happening to her.

Christa's lawyers fought the introduction of the skull into evidence. They insisted it was sensational and prejudicial. But Judge Leibowitz disagreed, believing that with the presentation of the skull, jurors could better understand the nature of the crime.

Looking up and speaking directly to the crowd, Leibowitz warned, "If there is any member of the audience that wishes to withdraw at this time, they are welcome to do so."

The returning jurors did not have the option. They took their places, prepared to hear the medical examiner's testimony.

Everyone in the courtroom dreaded the presentation of the skull. It was a macabre moment. Silence fell over the room. *Knoxville News-Sentinel* reporter John North waited with pen poised over paper. It would be only the second time in Knoxville history that a skull was ever introduced into evidence.

Numb and sick at heart, May and Raul elected to stay. They had wanted everyone to remember Colleen as the attractive, vivacious young woman she had been. Colleen's body had been cremated and her remains buried in Pennsylvania. Now to learn that the ashes in the grave might be incomplete was shocking news.

Jurors stared blankly as Dr. Elkins lifted the stark skull from a small box. Julie Martin leaned over to Christa and asked if she was all right. Christa nodded. Tears filled the young woman's eyes, then tumbled down her pale cheeks. Jurors didn't seem to notice the tears of the defendant; their eyes were fixed on the skull of her victim.

As Dr. Elkins gently held the skull of Colleen Slemmer in her hands, she explained how she had removed the entire brain before the head was amputated from the body.

A cold shiver ran down May's body. The courtroom suddenly felt as frosty as the late winter temperatures outside. Everyone, even the experienced reporters North and Belcher, was in shock.

"Was there anything that was located in the brain that you sent to the anthropology department with the skull?" Crabtree asked Dr. Elkins.

"Yes. There were multiple loose pieces of skull that were driven into the left side of the brain, and I removed as many of those pieces as possible. I sent those with the head to Dr. Murray Marks," Elkins explained.

With Dr. Elkins still holding Colleen's skull, Crabtree asked if she could indicate what type of weapon was used.

"Yes. Because there is still asphalt embedded in the skull," Elkins answered, pointing to an area of the skull cracked by the impact of rock against bone.

Crabtree produced a piece of bone and asked Dr. Elkins when she first saw this object.

"This past Friday was the first time I saw it in person," Elkins responded. "But I saw it photographically earlier."

"Was that piece of bone with the skull when you were doing the autopsy and removing the skull fragments?" Crabtree inquired.

"No."

"Can you say within a reasonable degree of medical certainty whether this piece of bone came from this skull that we are referring to?" Crabtree asked, holding up the bone fragment for jurors to see.

"Yes," the doctor replied.

Next, Crabtree displayed a small sack he designated as exhibit number nine. He asked Dr. Elkins to describe the contents for the jury.

Elkins took the small sack from Crabtree. "Within the sack, there are the top two cervical vertebra, the top two vertebra of the neck. And within here are several small skull fragments I removed from the deceased's brain, and fragments that Dr. Murray Marks was unable to fit—"

The medical examiner's testimony was interrupted by an objection from defense attorney Talman. "Your Honor, I would object to what Dr. Marks couldn't do. It is based on what he told her."

As testimony resumed, Dr. Elkins explained in a practiced monotone that the fragments taken

Colleen Anne Slemmer, 19.
(Photo courtesy Knox County, TN Criminal Court)

Tyson Park in Knoxville, Tennessee where Colleen Slemmer was murdered on Friday January 13, 1995.

The half-nude body of Colleen Slemmer was found on the edge
of the University of Tennessee campus by a groundskeeper.
(Photo courtesy Knox County, TN Criminal Court)

Slemmer's jacket was found twenty feet above her body snagged in the tree branches.
(*Photo courtesy Knox County, TN Criminal Court*)

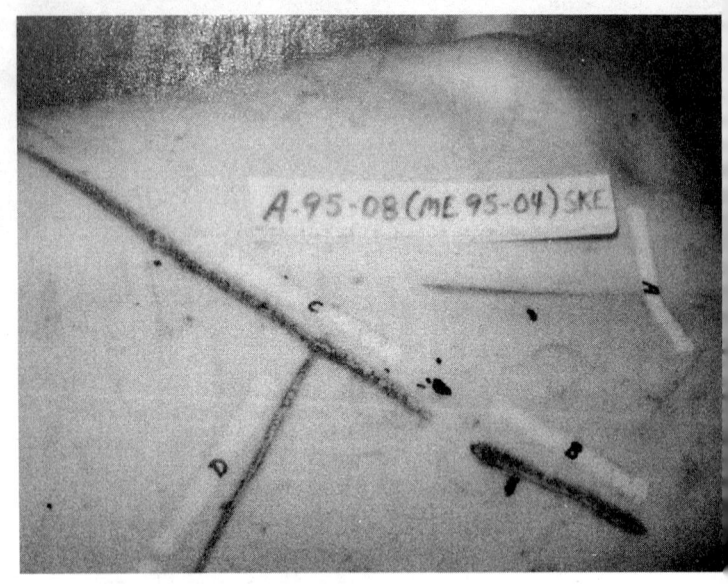

Slashes on Slemmer's back.
(*Photo courtesy Knox County, TN Criminal Court*)

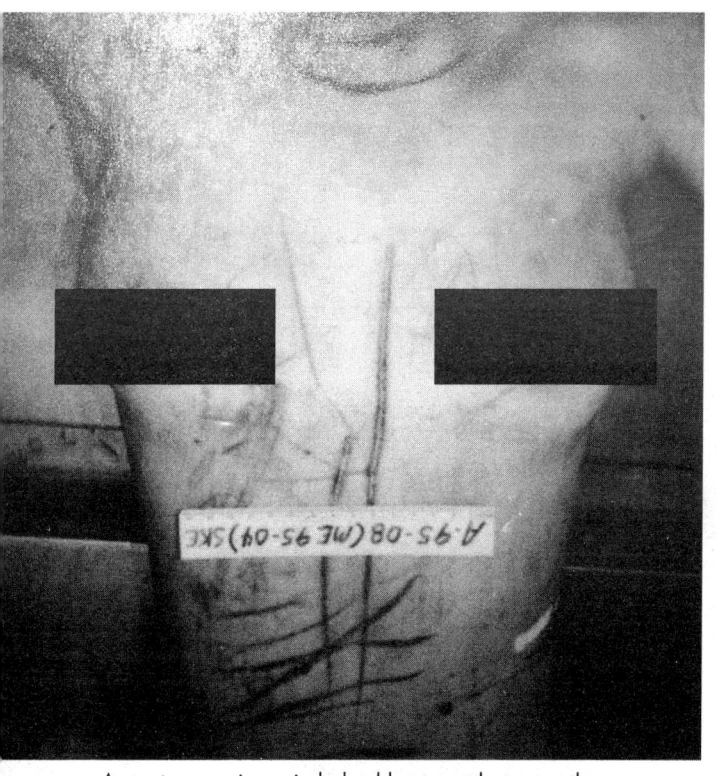

A pentagram in a circle had been cut between the victim's breasts with a box cutter.
(*Photo courtesy Knox County, TN Criminal Court*)

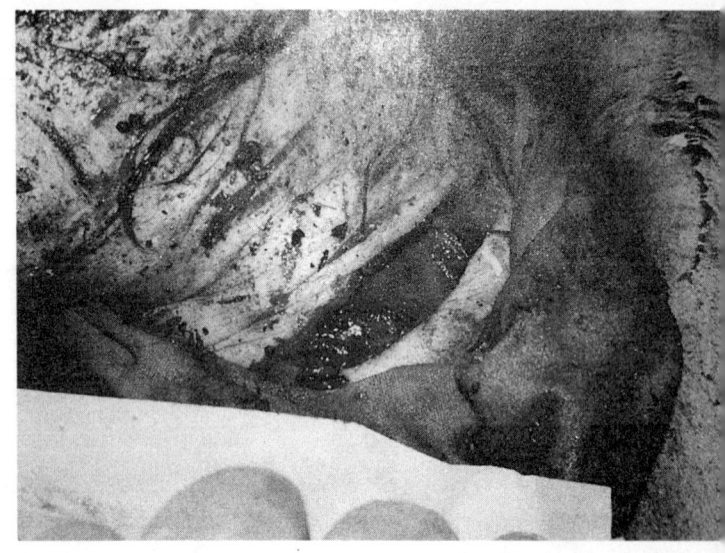

Slemmer's neck was slashed deeply enough
for the muscles to be visible.
("Photo courtesy Knox County, TN Criminal Court")

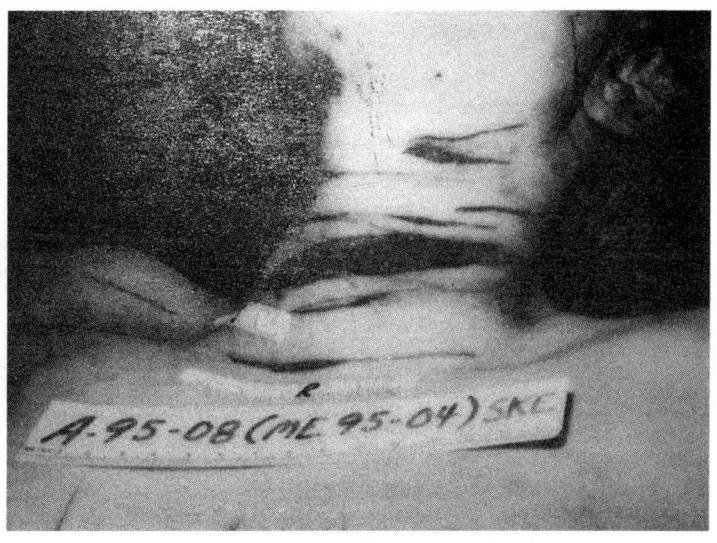

The gaping neck wound was six inches long.
(Photo courtesy Knox County, TN Criminal Court)

A blood-soaked rag was tied around Slemmer's deeply cut neck.
(Photo courtesy Knox County, TN Criminal Court)

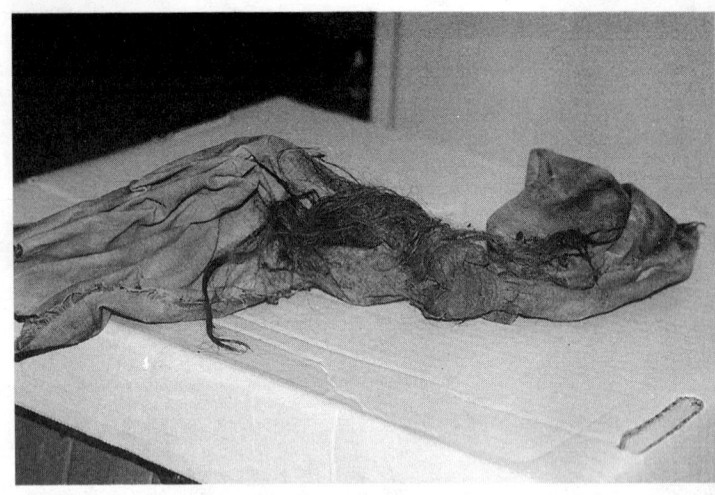

The rag used to gag Slemmer with a portion of
her hair still caught in the knot.
(*Photo courtesy Knox County, TN Criminal Court*)

The chunk of asphalt Christa Pike used to kill Colleen Slemmer.
(*Photo courtesy Knox County, TN Criminal Court*)

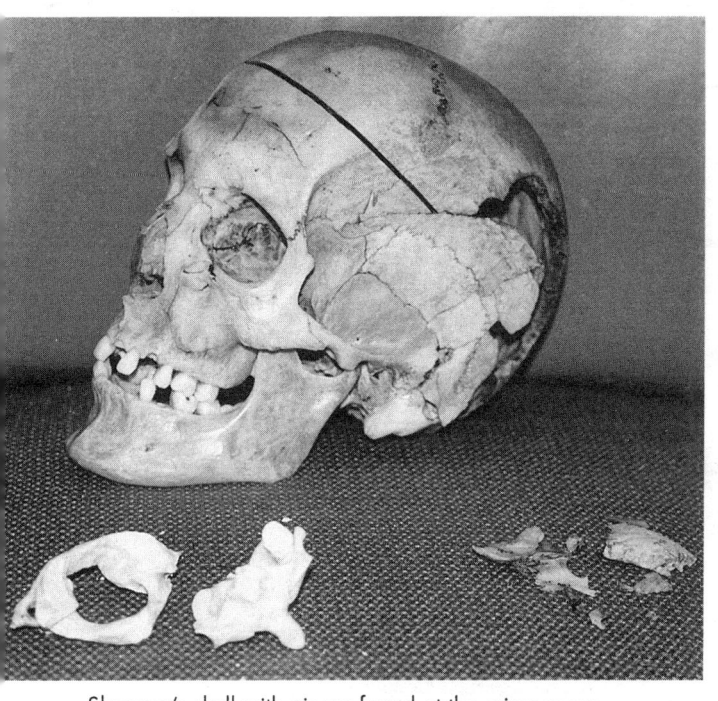

Slemmer's skull with pieces found at the crime scene.
(Photo courtesy Tennessee Court of Appeals)

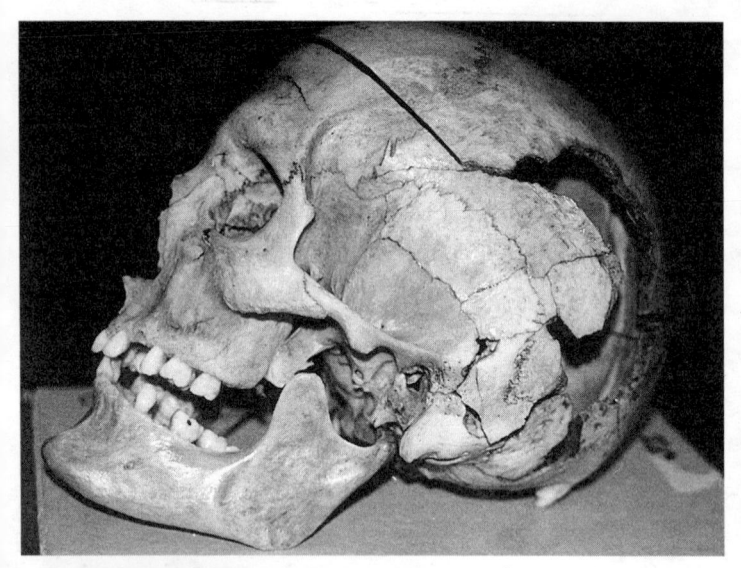

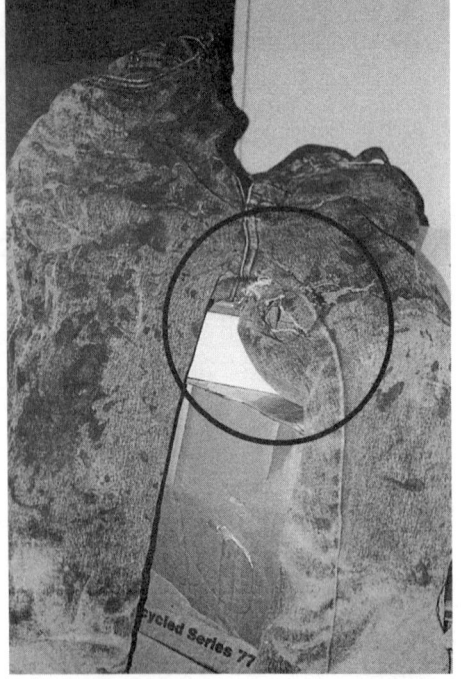

Close-up of skull shows the extent of damage done by Pike. (*Photo courtesy Tennessee court of Appeals*)

Slemmer's jeans with cuts made by Pike in the upper left leg near the crotch. (*Photo courtesy Knox County, TN Criminal Court*)

Christa Gale Pike, 18, received the death penalty for killing Colleen Slemmer.
(Photo courtesy Knox County, TN Sheriff's Office)

Knox county Courthouse where Colleen Slemmer's killers were sentenced.

Christa Pike crying in court as her taped confession is played for the jury. *(Photo courtesy Knoxville News-Sentinel)*

White circles on Pike's jacket indicate where human blood was found. A piece of Slemmer's skull was in a pocket. *(Photo courtesy Knox County, TN Criminal Court)*

Tadaryl Shipp, 17, was found guilty of first degree murder and sentenced to life in prison. *(Photo courtesy Knox County, TN Sheriff's Office)*

Shadolla Peterson, 18, plead guilty to accessory after the murder and was placed on probation. *(Photo courtesy Knox County, TN Sheriff's Office)*

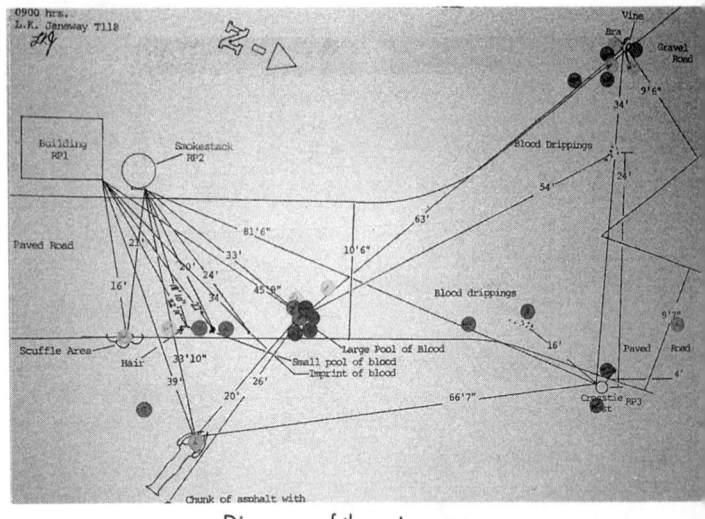

Diagram of the crime scene.
(Photo courtesy Knox County, TN Criminal Court)

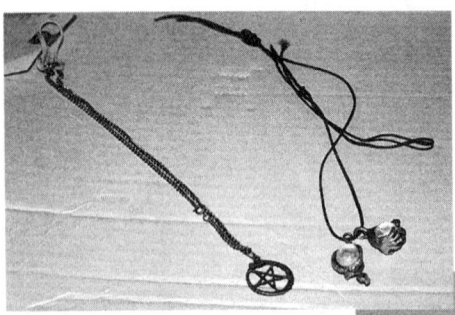

Necklace worn by Shipp. Pike wore an identical pentagram necklace. (Photo courtesy Knox County, TN Criminal Court)

Satanic statue found in Pike's room. (Photo courtesy Knox County, TN Criminal Court)

Smokestacks used by Christa Pike as point of reference to where she had attacked Slemmer.

Detective Randy York.

John North, reporter for the Knoxville *News-Sentinel*. (Photo courtesy Knoxville News-Sentinel)

Christa Pike is now on Tennessee's Death Row awaiting execution by lethal injection. (Photo courtesy Knox County, TN Sheriff's Office)

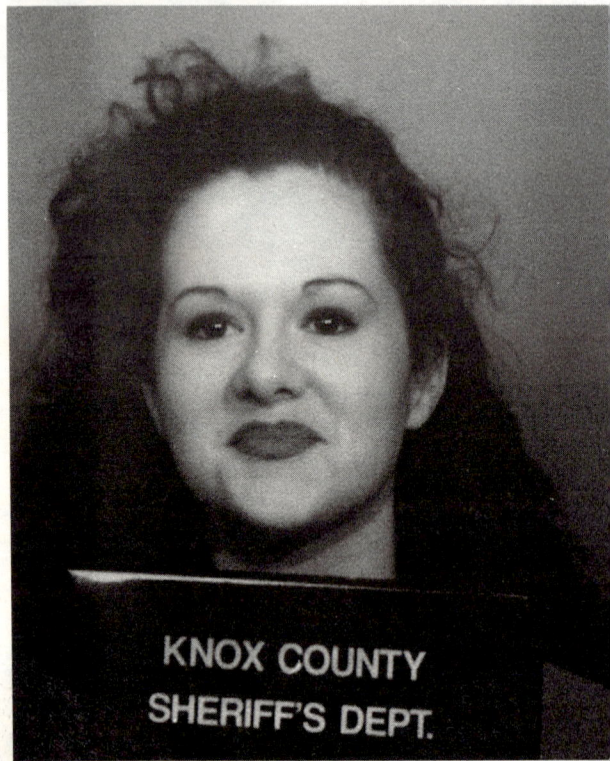

from the brain were glued back together where they fit properly into the skull.

"Like puzzle pieces," Judge Leibowitz commented.

"Right," Elkins acknowledged.

May shuddered slightly, chilled by the comparison of her daughter's skull to a table game.

Turning the back of the skull toward the jury, Elkins pointed out divots in the skull that still contained pieces of asphalt.

"This is the side of the head where the soft tissue was obscuring my view," Dr. Elkins said, pointing to the left side of the skull. "I knew that there was a large defect in the skull, and I wanted to know how many blows could have caused this damage to the left side of the head. Cleaning up the skull aided Dr. Marks and I in determining that there were at least two blows causing damage to the left side of the skull." In addition, Elkins pointed out more blackish particles embedded in the bone.

Dr. Elkins turned the skull forward as she began describing wounds to the front of the head. "There is a wound to the right brow area, and a wound up a bit higher on the skin. The wound in the brow area caused this fracture line running into the right eye socket and running across the front of the skull," Elkins said as she followed the crack with her finger.

May looked over at Christa, who had laid her head down on the defense table. Christa's torso rose and fell with each audible sniffle. May's glance strayed to Christa's mother, sitting behind her daughter in the gallery. She, too, had tears in her eyes. Although May knew they were hurting, her mercy was for Colleen, who had suffered from the blows the medical examiner so vividly described.

"Another wound, a blow to the nasal bridge that fractured the nasal bones, radiates out into both sides of the face. The blows to this side of head were with enough force that the skull split in two across the base of the skull. The brain would normally sit on that area. Fracturing the skull all the way across to the right side and up the right side is called a hinge fracture. That is what it is, a hinge," Elkins explained.

"What does that tell you?" Crabtree asked.

"The base of the skull fractures in the direction of the force. So when the base of the skull fractures across this way you know it's a side-to-side force. For the whole base to fracture and produce a hinge fracture to the side of the head not receiving the force, the head has to be against a solid object," Elkins expounded.

"Such as a roadway?" Crabtree inquired.

"Such as a roadway, or asphalt, or concrete," Elkins answered.

"And were you able to make a determination as to the cause of death?" Crabtree asked.

"Yes. Blunt force injuries to the head, or blows," Elkins responded.

"Up until those blows were actually inflicted on the victim, were any of the other injuries, wounds, lacerations, whatever, that you observed on the body sufficient to have caused death?" Crabtree probed.

"No."

"Were they sufficient to have caused a loss of consciousness in a relatively short period of time?" Crabtree continued to question.

"No."

"Would they have been painful, within a reasonable degree of medical certainty?" Crabtree persisted.

"Yes."

May lowered her head. Although she was suffering from the loss of Colleen and the anguish of sitting through the explanation of her daughter's torturous death, her heartache was nothing compared to the suffering Colleen had faced at the hands of the Christa Pike. May looked at the teenage defendant. Although Christa appeared remorseful, even tearful, May didn't believe for a minute that Christa regretted her actions—only where they had led her.

Dr. Elkins stepped down from the witness stand and stood before the jury. As instructed by the prosecutor, the doctor pointed out a crack in the skull that began above the left eye socket and ran in a line to the back of the head to a large gaping hole. Elkins indicated that this area was where various pieces of bone found embedded in the brain had originated.

While Crabtree had the pathologist close to the jury, he asked her to point out each of the skull fractures, making sure the jury could see them clearly. Again, she repeated the direction of the fractures, the damage each caused, and the position of the victim at the time of impact.

"Now, did this skull actually split into two parts?" Crabtree inquired, with emphasis on the last two words.

"Yes. It's in two parts because the base and the bottom of the skull have been completely fractured into a front and back half due to a strong force coming in from the side," Elkins responded.

"Does the skull tell you anything about the instrument that was used to inflict these blows?" Crabtree asked, attempting to introduce the murder weapon used to kill Colleen Slemmer. The doctor had already covered that, but Crabtree wanted to make absolutely sure that the jury understood the senseless violence used on Colleen Slemmer.

"Yes. At the time of autopsy, in the soft tissue surrounding this massive area of destruction on the left side of the skull, there were black firm particles within the soft tissue. Once the skull was processed and we were able to see the bone clearly, we could see two areas representing separate blows. If you look closely, you can see little divots in the skull. One of these divots retains a black particle. This is from the asphalt chunk that was used to administer the blows.

"From another blow you can see that a grayish black piece is embedded into the skull. Divots back here, one of them retaining one of these dark pieces," Elkins said, pointing to each of the places on the skull that contained the black foreign particles.

At the request of the prosecutor, Dr. Elkins again pointed out the four fractures in the skull: two blows to the left side of the skull caused a massive fracture; a separate blow impacted over the right eye; and another strike to the nose area, spreading into both sides of the face along the cheek region. Her words were repetitious, but very effective. The jury sat in shocked silence. No one spoke out. No one gasped. But the horror they understood could be seen in their eyes.

John North made notes in his notebook. Since he had been covering the Knox County courts, he had never seen a murder so despicable.

As Dr. Elkins returned to the witness chair, Judge Leibowitz asked the attorneys to approach the bench.

"That redheaded girl sitting by the jury looks as if she's getting sick," the judge informed the attorneys.

Other spectators in attendance were also feeling the effects of the graphic descriptions of the fatal blows that killed Colleen Slemmer, especially May Martinez. Despite her pain, she had no intention of leaving the courtroom. Nor did any of the other spectators. Each person continued to focus on the compelling testimony of the medical examiner.

"Can you give the minimum number of blows that were struck to the head?" Crabtree inquired.

"Taking into account soft tissue and skull, I could say that there were a minimum of five blows to the head," Elkins responded.

"You have described four blows, where was the fifth blow located?" Crabtree asked.

"There is an additional blow to the right forehead region. It did not cause a fracture in the skull itself, but injury to the soft tissue. Basically, I'm talking about the covering of the skull. The skin, some fat, and muscle," Elkins explained.

"When you were doing the autopsy and when you were removing this bone fragment from the brain, did that appear to be all of the bone that should have been there?" Crabtree explored.

"I wasn't sure. I suspected it was not. There is a very firm outer layer to the skull called the galea. It's a very thin, firm, almost ligamentous-type tissue that covers the skull. In most cases the galea will hold the pieces together when there is a fracture," Elkins answered.

"Has that been cleaned off this skull?" The prosecutor asked.

"Yes. It takes a lot of work, unless you chemically process the skull. It takes a great deal of scraping with a sharp edge which can distort your findings," Elkins responded.

May Martinez sat stone still, dazed by the testimony of the doctor. The head of her daughter had been displayed as though it was any inanimate object. The skull, with its cracks, holes, and missing teeth couldn't belong to her child. May remembered Colleen's happy smile and bright eyes. As she stared at the bony head, she could see in her memory Colleen's face, her overbite, and her funny little protruding lip. Her laughter. Her love. The skull held by Dr. Elkins, with its sharp jaw bone, bare eye sockets, and missing nose, bore no resemblance to the daughter May loved so much. She struggled to hold back tears.

"At the time of autopsy," Dr. Elkins testified, interrupting May's thoughts, "it seemed like there was a larger hole than the number of pieces of bone I recovered from the brain."

"I will show you what has been marked as exhibit ten and ask if you recognize that?" Crabtree said.

"Yes. I received that piece of skull this past Friday. I already had the skull. I took the piece and placed it where it belonged on the skull," Elkins responded.

As instructed by Crabtree, Dr. Elkins took the piece of bone from the clear plastic bag and placed it in the proper location of the skull. Jurors who were unable to see the bone and skull stood for a better view. The piece of bone fit perfectly into the vacant hole.

Assistant District Attorney Crabtree took the piece of bone from Dr. Elkins and carefully placed it back in the plastic bag. He wanted every member of the jury to remember that small piece of evidence with utter clarity. Much of the case against Christa Pike hinged on that small fragment of bone.

At Crabtree's request, Dr. Elkins again left the witness chair to stand in front of the fifteen jurors. Methodically, Crabtree had the medical examiner go over each of the lettered wounds for the jury. As the doctor spoke, she pointed to each wound in photographs that had been taken of the victim's body. Many of the jurors were visibly disturbed by the desecrated body of Colleen Slemmer. No warning by the court could have prepared them for what they were seeing.

Crabtree stopped the narration of wounds to ask Dr. Elkins to explain the bruising of the victim's body.

"As you can see on the right arm, as well as the right hand and elbow area, there are abrasions and contusions. As we move down the arm again, we have more bruises. Purple bruises. I always document what color the contusion is because, over a period of time, contusions, or bruises, change color. The first, fresh stage is purple. You see more bruising on the forearm, on the arm where the wrist area is, on down into the right hand itself. There are also abrasions and contusions on the back of the left hand," Elkins said in describing the wounds.

"Is there a forensic pathology name given to those type of wounds?" Crabtree asked.

"We call them defense wounds. Instinctively, we would all try to use our arms to shield off a weapon coming at us," Dr. Elkins stated.

A LOVE TO DIE FOR 137

May Martinez nodded slightly. She knew Colleen would have tried to defend herself. Colleen was a fighter. She always stood up for herself. But there was no way her daughter could have battled off the wrath of someone so determined to destroy her.

"There is another wound on the upper left-hand shoulder that you have labeled a slash, is that correct?" Crabtree asked.

"Yes. I did not give a letter to it," Elkins said, adding that there were innumerable superficial slash wounds on the back, arms, and chest of the victim that she did not label.

Members of the courtroom gallery shook their heads silently, asking themselves how Christa Pike could have performed such torture, as well as how Colleen Slemmer could have lived through it.

Dr. Elkins resumed her classification of the injuries. Crabtree had the pathologist explain the reddish mark on the upper right-hand part of the torso.

"Those are basically scrapes or abrasions," Elkins explained, indicating that the marks could have been made by the victim being dragged across an asphalt surface by her feet. And again, Elkins told jurors that Colleen was alive at the time the abrasions were made.

"As you began to clean the body, did a pattern begin to emerge?" Crabtree asked, setting up a response he felt certain would shock the jurors.

"I immediately saw on the chest, between the

breasts, a very specific pattern to those slash or incised wounds of the skin. It was what most people refer to as a pentagram. A five-pointed star in a circle," Elkins responded.

Crabtree had guessed right. The eyes of some jurors widened at the description of the pattern cut into Colleen's chest. Muffled gasps could be heard from spectators.

Photos of the cuts on Colleen's chest were circulated in the jurors' box. Most jurors sat stone faced and stared at the grotesque pictures. Others twisted nervously in their blue-upholstered chairs.

"You've made a notation on this photograph, Doctor. What is the significance of the notation?" Crabtree wanted to know.

"Mud with drag marks on the right of the torso. They were very distinctive. You could tell there were linear etches in the mud, representing where the body had been dragged through it," Elkins said, explaining her findings.

Crabtree continued Elkins's exhaustive testimony by having her explain the unlettered wounds to the face and neck, [as well as the blunt force injuries labeled "U," "V," and "W" to the head.] Elkins told the court that Colleen sustained ten slash wounds to the neck, including the gaping incise wound labeled "S." For the third time, she noted that the neck wounds were made by two different instruments, and a third weapon used to perform the blunt force trauma. Again, Crabtree had his witness emphasize that Colleen Slemmer was alive during the brutal attack.

Crabtree paused, then seized a large brown paper bag from near the prosecution table, and carefully removed a pair of blood- and mud-stained blue jeans. Dr. Elkins confirmed they were the jeans taken from the victim prior to the autopsy.

May swallowed hard. They were the jeans she had given Colleen the summer before she left for the Job Corps, along with the sweater she was wearing the night she was killed. It was one of the most painful moments of the trial for May.

"Is this the condition they were in when you removed them?" Crabtree asked.

"Well, they weren't this dry, but yes, they had the tear here," Elkins answered, pointing to the cut in the garment at the upper right thigh.

"Your Honor, rather than passing this, I will just walk down and hold these up for the jury to see," Crabtree stated.

Slowly, Crabtree passed in front of the jury box so that each juror could see the dark red bloodstains, the muddy smudges, and the fabric cuts. The garment was a shocking visual display of the horror Colleen Slemmer must have suffered. The blood, the mud, even the cut in the leg of her pants, revealed her struggle for life.

Then Crabtree presented the blood-soaked cloth that had been tied in a knot, caught in Colleen's hair, and cut from the body by Dr. Elkins as exhibit number twenty-one. May Martinez looked at the cloth with understanding in her eyes. Colleen would naturally have cursed, yelled, even pleaded with her attackers. She understood why Colleen had been gagged.

Dr. Elkins's testimony was complete. She had been invaluable to the prosecution. Crabtree felt that Elkins's detailed delineation of the wounds helped jurors envision the carnage suffered by Colleen Slemmer. Her fight for life. Her will to live. Her final defeat.

Crabtree, a twenty-year veteran of the District Attorney's Office, felt in command of the trial. But the feeling of control vanished minutes later when the trial was halted. The jury and spectators looked questioningly at one another, not understanding what was happening, but the prosecution did. The defense was trying a new ploy to stop the trial. In an unprecedented move, the defense attorneys had subpoenaed all twenty-five Knox County prosecutors, including Crabtree and Helm. Court officials were stunned.

"With the permission of the court, we would like to be permitted to withdraw from this case," Knox County Assistant District Attorney General Bill Crabtree told Judge Leibowitz, as he struggled to suppress his anger.

With no prosecutors in court or in the building who hadn't been subpoenaed, no one was left to contest the motion. Leibowitz had no option. The trial was suspended.

Twelve

The confusion causing the unscheduled recess in the capital murder trial of Christa Pike had been prompted by defense attorney William Talman. Talman and co-counsel Julie Martin had learned that Knox County Sheriff Deputies Tim DeBord, Jeanette Harris, and Charles Price had overheard a conversation Talman considered privileged between Pike and her former attorney, William Brown. The blanket subpoena was an effort to learn if the deputies had been instructed by prosecutors to listen to conversations between Pike and Brown in order to gain information against Pike.

Confused spectators wondered what Pike could have said to her attorney that she had not already stated in her oral confession obtained by police and reported in the *Knoxville News-Sentinel*.

"I heard Ms. Pike make the statement. I know what I did was wrong," sheriff's deputy, Lieutenant Tim DeBord testified, believing that he had unintentionally breached the client-attorney privilege between Pike and Brown.

Two other Knox County officers also testified they'd heard a distraught Christa Pike make the statement—a statement known only to those privy to the conversation.

"The exchange between Pike and Brown was protected by attorney-client privilege," Talman argued.

"When a third party is present, particularly uniformed sheriff's officers, there is no privilege," Crabtree countered angrily. He was convinced that the privileged communication between a client and his attorney, which allows immunity from legal process for the contents of the conversation, had not been violated.

Judge Leibowitz agreed.

Spectators were left wondering what Christa Pike had said to William Brown in the jail corridor.

May and Raul roamed the halls of the City-County Building waiting for the trial to resume. May looked out the expanse of second-floor windows. Construction was underway in many parts of the downtown area. New commercial buildings were being erected beside historic structures restored to their former grander. Residences and commercial establishments were intermingled. City streets were being reworked to re-create the historical atmosphere. Knoxville was a thriving municipality.

Raul stroked his salt-and-pepper beard, looking at his wife, wishing he could ease her pain. May hated having to be in the city by the river. She wanted to go home to Florida. But May and Raul would remain in Knoxville until the trial was over. Until Christa Pike was punished.

As the Tennessee state flag—a red field with three white stars in a blue circle, edged on the right side with a narrow white band and a broader blue band—whipped in the wind outside the City-County Building, Assistant State Attorney General John H. Baker III arrived at the front. Baker was soon in the third-floor criminal courtroom to represent the state in the absence of any eligible assistant district attorney of Knox County. He officially asked that the motion made by Talman be quashed. Judge Leibowitz complied and ordered the proceedings resumed.

But trial testimony would have to wait. Crabtree was infuriated by the disruption and what he called "a blatant abuse of process" by the defense.

His fair complexion flushed from anger, Crabtree approached the bench. "I request that the costs of the subpoenas be paid by Mr. Talman and Ms. Martin, not the county," Crabtree told Judge Leibowitz, obviously irritated by the defense's surprise ploy.

The cost for each of the twenty-five subpoenas issued was ten dollars and fifty cents. If all summons were delivered, the cost incurred by the county would total two hundred sixty-two dollars and fifty cents. Leibowitz concurred with Crabtree; his office should not be saddled with the expense of a frivolous act by the defense.

Talman, a short, stocky man with a receding hairline and metal-rimmed glasses, approached the bench. He apologized to Judge Leibowitz, but added that he intended to appeal her ruling. The threat of appeal failed to deter Leibowitz. She instantly called the court to order.

After the hour-long interruption, the trial finally resumed, with Robert Pollock of the Knoxville Job Corps taking the stand. Assistant District Attorney Helms held the black jacket belonging to Christa Pike in her hands as she approached the witness.

"I object, Your Honor," Talman said, standing to address the court. The defense counsel argued that it had not been proven that the jacket belonged to Pike.

"The state will offer evidence showing that the coat was Pike's," the fifty-something female prosecutor responded.

Based on the assumption that the state would show a connection between Pike and the black leather jacket held by Helms, Judge Leibowitz allowed the testimony to continue.

Pollock stated that on January 13, 1995, at about 3:15 P.M., Christa Pike came to his office to have a new identification card made.

"There were ten to twelve students there," Pollock explained. "Christa sat in the first chair by the door."

Helms asked the Job Corps worker if he recalled what Christa was wearing.

"She had on a light-colored top and some jewelry. Christa left her black, short leather jacket hanging on the back of the chair," Pollock stated.

"What happened to that jacket?" Helms asked.

"I locked the room at 4:05 P.M. When I returned on January seventeenth the jacket was still there. I took it to security," Pollock said.

"Was anyone with Christa when she was at your office?" Helms inquired.

"Tadaryl Shipp was with her on the thirteenth," Pollack responded.

"Did she appear upset?" Helms asked.

"No."

"Frightened?"

"No."

"Crying?"

"No," Pollock answered.

Christa folded a piece of paper she had been writing on, turned toward the gallery, and passed it to her mother. May watched the two exchange smiles. It made her angry to see Christa and her mother together, even if separated by a wooden railing. It made her miss Colleen even more.

As Christa turned to focus her attention on the testimony at hand, her gaze fell on the handsome television reporter, Charley Belcher. Christa smiled, blinking her eyes in a flirtatious way. Belcher recognized the familiar gaze. A slight smiled curved the outer edges of his lips. It seemed he and Christa were developing an unspoken rapport. It would be useful if he were to secure an interview later.

William Hudson, manager of safety and security at the Job Corps Center told jurors he was given the jacket by Pollock after hearing of Pike's arrest. Hudson called the Knoxville Police Department to report the jacket in his possession.

"I didn't search the jacket," Hudson stated, adding that he turned the jacket over to criminalistics specialist Arthur Bohanan of the KPD.

Bohanan testified that, four days after the murder of Colleen Slemmer, he was summoned to the office of William Hudson, on the west side of the Job Corp campus. At that time Hudson gave a jacket to Bohanan, telling him it belonged to Christa Pike.

"I searched the three pockets of the jacket Hudson gave me," Bohanan told jurors. "In the right front pocket I found some cough drops. The left front pocket was empty. In the inside left breast pocket I found a fork, a cigarette butt, and a small piece of bone."

The officer's testimony was short and to the point. A piece of bone had been found in Christa Pike's jacket pocket. Everyone in the courtroom immediately thought of the bone fragment Dr. Elkins had earlier inserted into Colleen Slemmer's skull. The piece had fit perfectly.

Christa smiled sweetly at the man the state called as a new witness. Dr. Murray Marks was tall, dark haired, attractive, and well dressed in a white shirt, patterned tie, and dark suit. Reporters noticed that the tears Christa had cried during Dr. Elkins's testimony had dried up. They also caught the almost saucy look she had given the new witness.

Marks took the oath to tell the truth, then settled into the witness chair for questioning by Crabtree.

Dr. Marks, an anthropologist at the University of Tennessee, explained to the court that he processed the skull by soaking it in a mixture of hot water, mild detergent, and bleach for three to four hours. He dissected as much of the soft tissue as possible.

"The processing doesn't take long on a skull because the tissue, a fibrous coating adjacent to the bone, is thin," Dr. Marks explained. "It took several hours for the soft tissue to fall away, and two hours to dry."

Crabtree asked the doctor what he found once the skull had been processed.

"After the remains were in a state to where I could examine the skeletal injury, I found two main areas that had injury. The left-side area behind the ear and some fracturing on the front of the face," Marks stated.

"Prior to your reconstruction, how did the skull appear?" Crabtree inquired.

"There were about seven or eight pieces that were missing along this line," Marks said, pointing to a large open area on the skull. "And I believe one or two pieces that were missing along the side region here."

The jurors' eyes were fixated on the skull in Dr. Marks's hands. He handled the skeletal remains confidently, yet gently.

May Martinez shifted uneasily in her place on the front-row bench. It took all the willpower she could muster to watch another doctor handle her daughter's remains. But she was determined to stay through every heart-wrenching, gut-twisting minute of the trial.

"Your Honor, may I have him step down?" Crabtree asked.

"Sure," Leibowitz answered.

"Please bring the skull with you," Crabtree instructed Marks. "Now, if you would, sir, concerning this area across through here. What is that caused by?" Crabtree referred to the circular cut around the skull.

"That is a result of autopsy," Marks stated.

"Would you just show the jury how big a hole there was in the side of the skull?" Crabtree asked the anthropologist.

Dr. Marks pointed out a large area on the left back of the skull.

"And that is the area that you filled in when you did the reconstruction, is that correct?" Crabtree inquired.

"That's correct. There's probably about seven or eight, maybe as many as ten pieces reconstructed in the skull," Marks explained.

Dr. Marks continued by saying that the pieces used to do the reconstruction had been contained in the soft tissue. He pointed out trauma sustained to the front of the head, including the nasal bone. The doctor clarified for jurors that the fracture on the right side of the head was not a result of impact trauma, but was sustained as a result of the head being against a hard surface at the time the opposite side of the head was struck. His words supported everything Dr. Elkins had said earlier.

Dr. Marks resumed his seat in the witness box.

"Now, Dr. Marks, as a result of your observations of the skull, and I am talking about from the bone only, and not from soft tissue, can you tell us the minimum number of blows that this head received?" Crabtree asked.

"The minimum number of blows to the skull was at least four," Marks answered.

"Is there anything embedded in this skull?" Crabtree questioned.

"There is a small piece of some type of rocklike material that's embedded in this region of the bone," Marks said, pointing to an area, adding that there were more perforations and pitting in other areas of the bone.

"Would that be consistent with, say, asphalt?" Crabtree asked.

"Could be. Yes."

"Now, after you had received this skull, processed it, done the reconstruction, did you have an occasion to see another piece of bone?" Crabtree asked, setting Dr. Marks up for the final question.

"Yes, sir," Marks responded.

"And who did you receive that from?" Crabtree queried.

"It came from Arthur Bohanan," Marks stated.

The setup was perfect. Crabtree could now connect the bone Bohanan had found in the pocket of Christa Pike's jacket to the skull of Colleen Slemmer. Crabtree paused dramatically before asking his witness if the bone fit in the skull of the victim.

"No doubt whatsoever. It fit the skull," Dr. Marks said with absolute assurance.

Carefully holding the skull of Colleen Slemmer in his large hands, Crabtree slipped the piece of bone into a hole on the left side of the skull. Again, the piece fit snugly.

Thirteen

On the third day of the trial, Christa Pike entered the courtroom with the usual cheerful smile and timid wave to her mother. The forensic evidence presented by Drs. Elkins and Marks was finally over. Christa appeared more relaxed, totally unaware that this would be her most difficult day in court.

Christa's mood changed abruptly and she glared at the young woman who took the witness stand. Kimberly Iloilo had been one of Christa's friends at the Job Corps Center, but now she was helping the state in their effort to convict her.

Kimberly nervously brushed her dark hair back from her naturally tanned face. She began by telling the court that she had known Christa, Colleen, Shadolla, and Tadaryl for three or four months before the killing.

"Christa and I talked about Colleen in her room the evening of January eleventh, the day before the murder. Christa said she was going to kill Colleen," Kimberly stated. Her dark Hawaiian eyes avoided looking at the defendant, as she nervously wrung her hands.

Reporters who recalled the opening statement of defense attorney Julie Martin wondered how the defense would get around the premeditation question after Kimberly's testimony. Her statement seemed to show that Christa had indeed planned to kill Colleen before they ever arrived at Tyson Park.

"The night of the murder, I saw Colleen, Christa, Tadaryl, and Shadolla leave the Job Corps campus together about eight P.M. A little over two hours later, I saw everyone return. Everyone except Colleen. I never saw Colleen again," Kimberly said, keeping her eyes fixed on the prosecutor, escaping Christa's cold stare.

Kimberly told the court that later on the night of the murder, Christa came to her dorm room to talk.

"She said, 'First, you can't say anything. Okay? I just killed Colleen Slemmer.' She told me that she killed Colleen, cut her throat, and beat her up. She said she had thrown asphalt at her head," Kimberly said, her voice shaking.

"She said they kept cutting her throat because she was a witch, and because she was still talking. They were trying to stop her from talking."

Kimberly described to spectators in the small courtroom how Christa danced around in a circle as she told her the story of the killing. "She was smiling and singing 'La-la-la-la-la,'" Kimberly said.

As blood rushed to May Martinez's cheeks, her eyes narrowed. She was sickened by the pleasure killing Colleen seemed to have brought to Christa. Again, she wondered what had turned her into a cold-blooded killer, and why she seemingly derived such pleasure from it.

The filled courtroom gasped as they heard Kimberly tell the jury that the following morning at breakfast, Christa told her she had a piece of Colleen's skull in her pocket. "I'm eating breakfast with it," Christa had told Kimberly.

With the image of the shattered skull and the missing piece of bone described by both Dr. Marks and Dr. Elkins in their minds, as well the vivid description of Christa taking the bone fragment to the breakfast table, the prosecution turned the witness over to the defense for cross-examination.

"When she told you she was going to kill Colleen, what did you do about it?" Talman asked Kimberly.

Kimberly stated that there were four students in the dorm room when Christa made the comment. "We blew it off as soon as it was said. We didn't take her seriously. She was calm when it was said," Kimberly explained.

Still avoiding Christa's scowl, Kimberly told the jury that she was in shock when Christa told her about the killing. She didn't want to believe it was true. She didn't want to believe Colleen was really dead.

May sat in silence. Perhaps Colleen's murder

could have been avoided if only Kimberly had taken Christa's threats seriously. But she couldn't blame Kimberly. Christa was the one responsible for Colleen's death. Christa had plunged the asphalt against the head of her daughter. And Christa would have to pay.

Christa watched in silence as Kimberly was dismissed, and another of her Job Corps classmates took the witness stand. The sweet, almost angelic expression on Christa's face had disappeared. A cold hard stare had taken its place.

Stephanie Wilson had been in class with Christa the morning after the murder and Christa had told her that what appeared to be mud on her shoes, was really blood. The blood of Colleen Slemmer.

"Then she said she had something to show me. She pulled a napkin out of her jacket. She opened it and said it was a piece of a human skull. I asked her whose and she said Colleen Slemmer's," Stephanie stated.

The gallery appeared unshaken. They were beginning to realize that Christa was proud of her deed, even boastful, but they could not understand the enjoyment she seemingly derived by taking another life. A few onlookers shook their heads, indicating confusion.

"Christa said she and Tadaryl went walking and she slashed Colleen's throat six times. She said she beat her in the head with a rock and took a piece of her skull. She said blood and brains were pouring out as she hit her in the head. That was it. Christa said it was a spur of the moment thing because she just felt like it," Stephanie testified.

Through the testimony of the two Job Corps students, Crabtree had managed to paint Christa Pike as a cold-blooded, remorseless killer. Christa Pike herself would be his most damning witness.

Detective Randy York strolled to the stand with confidence, his dark hair complemented by his dark jacket. The case he had put together for the District Attorney's Office against Christa Pike was solid. He felt self-assured as he recounted his activities of the morning of January 13, 1995, when he first arrived at the crime scene.

May Martinez liked York. He had kept her informed of the progress of his investigation of her daughter's murder during the year since she had lost Colleen. She had confidence in him to strike a blow to the defense that would be insurmountable.

York told jurors that after a tip from an informant, he went to the Job Corps campus to speak to Christa Pike. "She said she'd give a statement under certain conditions. That she wouldn't have to mention who else was with her," York testified.

Then York provided some of the most wrenching moments yet in the first-degree-murder trial. For the next hour and ten minutes, jurors and courtroom spectators heard a weepy, sometimes defiant Christa Gail Pike detail the slaughter of

Colleen Slemmer on a tape recording made by York on the day following the murder.

The tension in the courtroom was palpable. No movement. No rustling. It was if a Polaroid picture had frozen the courtroom in time. Waiting. Anticipating the words of Christa Pike.

Christa stated that Colleen had given her a lot of problems. She claimed to have awakened one night at the Job Corps with Slemmer standing over her with a box cutter. She also admitted that in the few months she had been at the Job Corps, she had been in trouble with school authorities.

The young defendant began by talking of hitting and beating Colleen, adding how angry Colleen had made her on the night of the murder.

"She wouldn't shut up," Christa was heard saying on the tape. "She kept talking and talking. She would start talking again, and I would say, 'Shut up.' I didn't want to hear her talking."

Colleen's mother bit her lower lip, forcing back tears as she heard her daughter's murderer confess on tape.

"The other person was over there screaming at her and screaming at her. He was in her face, you know. She had blood all over her, covering her whole face all the way down her shirt. Well, not down her shirt—she didn't have her shirt on. We had made her take off her shirt when she was sitting up. She had on a bra and jeans and socks and shoes. It was a sweater, pink or something," Christa's voice said on the tape.

Sick at heart, May swallowed the bile that rose

in her throat. She asked herself, how could these kids see all the blood, the kicking, the screaming, the cutting, and sleep with it?

"I thought maybe if I stripped her naked, maybe she wouldn't get up and run. I didn't want anybody to see her, you know. Her bra was cut off and it was still hanging on her arm. When she took off running is when I cut her down her back. It turned bright where I cut her, then it started bleeding. It was like, 'Oh, my God, what did I do?' I started thinking more and more, how I gotta get myself outta this. I got to get myself outta this because I'm not going to be able to handle it, you know.

"Colleen started looking at me, going, why the hell are you doing this to me? She just started going off and going off. She started grabbing at me and everything. She was laying in this pool of blood and I was just looking at her," continued the tape.

The courtroom remained silent. No one moved. No one spoke. It was as if everyone had been transported to that secluded service road behind the university power plant. They could see Colleen Slemmer lying in the pool of blood. Hear her cries. Feel her pain.

"I was scared," Christa said, but there was no emotion in her taped voice. "I was like, 'Oh, my God, what in the hell is wrong with me? What's wrong with her? What's wrong with everybody?' I still had the box cutter in my hand and I cut her across the throat with it. It didn't go deep.

It didn't even bleed for a long time. Then it started bleeding and I was like, 'Oh, my God.' She wasn't dead. She just kept talking and talking and talking. What was wrong with her? I was thinking, 'I just sliced her throat, what's wrong with her?' She started staring at me."

Christa described for spellbound courtroom attendees how white Slemmer's skin had seemed right after she cut her, just before the blood began to flow.

May could no longer hold back the tears. The oral confession of Christa was too much to endure. The strength of Colleen, her will to live, had amazed Christa, and infuriated her.

" 'You need to fuckin' talk to me,' she kept saying. She was sitting up because we had pushed her down on the ground. Then she would get back up and we'd push her down. For about thirty minutes to an hour. Finally, she was just laying there.

"One time she took off running and I picked up a rock and threw it at her, 'cause I knew I couldn't catch her. I threw it at her and hit her in the back of the head with it. She fell. Her head was bleeding. This other person hit her with a rock. Then she was like, I could hear how she was breathing. She was like breathing blood in and out. Kind of gurgling. She was jumping and jerking. I just kept hitting her and hitting her and hitting her. She was still breathing, you know. She wasn't talking anymore."

Wide-eyed jurors listened intently as the

graphic, gut-wrenching tape continued to play. They kept their eyes affixed to the transcripts of the taped confession handed them by Crabtree moments before the tape began to play. John North was stunned. He had never covered such a horrific murder for the newspaper. Charley Belcher knew his first story for WATE-TV was one he would never forget.

Christa was insistent that she had not taken a piece of Colleen's skull as a souvenir.

"Why would I want a piece of her skull?" Christa could be heard saying on tape.

"Did you take a piece of it?" York asked.

"That's disgusting. No, I did not," Christa stated flatly.

But jurors had heard the testimony, and seen the bone fragment. They knew Christa was lying.

"I said, 'Colleen, do you know what's doing this to you?'" Christa sounded tearful as she spoke to York the day after Slemmer's body was found in a remote area of the University of Tennessee Agricultural campus. Then Christa added, "She only moaned in reply."

Everyone present at the trial sat in silent horror. The courtroom was quiet, but the words of Christa Pike continued to ring in everyone's ears: "She only moaned . . ."

At the end of the long, painful recording, a few of the jurors looked over at Christa, who was sniffling into a tissue, sitting stooped between her lawyers.

Christa, who would turn twenty in two weeks,

then put her head down on the defense table and sobbed. Her torso rose and fell heavily as the tears rolled from her eyes. But Christa was not alone in her sorrow. Her mother cried as well, as did the mother of her victim. Both women had lost their daughters. One to murder, one to jealousy.

The forensic evidence had been wrenching, but nothing compared to Christa's own words. Her statement gave prosecutors the most damning evidence to ensure a conviction.

With York still in the witness box, Crabtree approached the bench and handed a copy of the confession signed by Christa to Judge Leibowitz for admission.

"What's that notation?" the judge asked York.

York took the document from the judge and studied it carefully. "It says, 'Litl Devil,' " York told Judge Leibowitz, denoting that the reference was to Christa's nickname.

"No, what do the numbers under the signature mean?" the Judge asked.

Again, York considered the document carefully before responding. "I don't know, Your honor, I'm unfamiliar with those numbers. I never noticed them before."

Scrawled under the signature of Christa Pike and her nickname, "Litl Devil" were the numbers 2-4-26. York knew that couldn't possibly be the nineteen-year-old's date of birth. He was stumped. Not until later would York learn the significance of the numbering. Two plus four equals six; four plus two equals six; and the final character six all represented the satanic symbol 666. Followers of Satan believed that 666 was used to identify an individual as a child of the devil. Christa Pike evidently saw herself as one of Satan's children.

After the brief delay, York continued with his testimony. "Christa told me about a pair of blue jeans in her room that had blood on them. She said she rubbed mud on them to cover up. She gave us a consent to search and we found them folded in her room."

Christa seemed to have regained her composure once the oral statement had finished. With red eyes and tear-streaked cheeks, she watched York closely as he continued his testimony.

"She told us about the items discarded at the Texaco Station at Twenty-second and Cumberland. They were in a garbage can inside the women's bathroom," York said.

Then the jurors and spectators heard a bone-chilling description by York of Christa's reenactment of the murder.

"I wanted to video Christa's declaration, so I asked her to retrace her steps from the night of the murder. She took us up Seventeenth Street to a side street, then out to an area she called "the strip," which is Cumberland Avenue, and on to Tyson Park. When we arrived at the area where the body was found, she told me what happened," York informed jurors.

"Christa was very animated during the video

taping at the crime scene," York said, adding that Christa portrayed both her part as the murderer, and Colleen's role as the victim.

The scenario York described was of a remorseless murderer, playing out the brutal killing of Colleen Slemmer as if it were a high school play being performed for a second time. As York described the scene, Christa pulled her white sweater closer to her body. Tears once again dampened her cheeks.

There seemed little left for Crabtree and Helm to do. Christa's own words most likely had sealed the conviction, but Crabtree wanted to make certain that there was no question in the minds of jurors just who was responsible for Colleen's death.

The state called Raymond DePriest of the Tennessee Bureau of Investigation Forensic Serology and DNA Analysis Unit. The blood specialist produced the jacket belonging to Christa Pike. White circles, from a paint marker, dotted the black leather.

"The white paint marker showed red and brown stains found on the jacket. The stains tested positive for human blood," DePriest stated. Although the expert was unable to match the blood with Colleen Slemmer's, the visual impression of the dotted jacket, combined with York's previous testimony, clearly gave jurors a reasonable assumption that the bloodstains indeed belonged to Colleen. They studied the garment carefully.

"I also tested a pair of Fila tennis shoes," DePriest told attentive jurors. "There was reddish-brown staining across the tops of the shoes, intertwined in the laces. There was one conclusive test for human blood."

After explaining the blood found on clothing belonging to Tadaryl Shipp, DePriest indicated that blood splatters were also found, front and bottom, on the jeans belonging to Christa Pike.

In three days, prosecutors had presented an overwhelming amount of evidence against Christa Pike. But the most incriminating information facing the teen remained her own words: "Colleen, do you know what's doing this to you?"

The state rested its case.

Fourteen

Christa Pike sat animated, almost bubbly, as the Knox County Criminal Court trial shifted to the defense, with Dr. Eric S. Engum called as the first witness. As the clinical psychologist walked to the stand, Christa turned and waved at Charley Belcher. For several days, Christa had been flashing an occasional smile at Belcher during recess breaks and during trial proceedings. Her impulsive actions were interpreted by some as a sign of a lack of remorse, even brashness. Strange behavior for someone fighting for her life.

As Dr. Engum's testimony began, he stated that he had visited with Christa in May 1995, four months after her arrest. Engum found Christa to be extremely bright, with excellent problem-solving skills, and fairly remarkable cognitive abilities. Although she'd only completed the ninth grade, Christa registered 111 on her IQ test. In addition to the intelligence exam, the psychologist had administered four personality tests to Christa, the results leading him to a diagnosis of severe borderline personality disorder.

"Christa has a multiplicity of problems in interpersonal relationships and in controlling her behavior," Engum told the court. "She has difficulty achieving vocational and academic kinds of goals."

Judge Leibowitz shifted her gaze from the doctor in the witness chair to Christa. The defendant seemed unaffected by the psychologist's testimony. Leibowitz thought she even detected a slight smirk on the accused's face.

The judge studied Christa with interest. Then their eyes met. Suddenly, Christa's demeanor changed. The small smile faded and her face became drawn and sorrowful. Her shoulders drooped and her chin lowered. Could Christa be putting on a remorseful act for the court? An act she hoped would spare her life? Leibowitz's attention returned to Engum's testimony.

"Ms. Pike has a highly unstable identity. She basically draws her identity from those around her. She is highly dependent on others because she has so little sense of self. She has a severe fear of abandonment by those important to her. She may fall deeply in love, but is always frantic that person will leave or abandon her. She is always looking for signs to confirm their love. She will do anything to maintain that love relationship," Dr. Engum told jurors.

"Christa fell deeply, deeply in love with Shipp. Her fear of losing him, her fear of having him taken by the victim was so threatening, so overwhelming, it caused a huge reaction. She saw Colleen as a direct threat to her ability to maintain her relationship with Tadaryl," Engum explained.

May Martinez shook her head. She knew Colleen was no threat to Christa and Tadaryl. She knew her daughter's preference in boys, and Tadaryl was definitely not someone Colleen would be attracted to. Christa had misinterpreted the signs. If only she had listened to Colleen's denial in regard to Tadaryl.

Engum shifted slightly in his chair and continued his explanation of Christa's mental status. "People with borderline personality disorder are in love one minute and angry, bitter, hostile, and resentful the next because of the perception of being abandoned. Their emotions swing alternately and are very unpredictable. This is reflective of Pike throughout her life."

Tears accumulated in Carissa Hansen's eyes. They tumbled down her cheeks as she stared at her childlike daughter sitting at the defense table. What part had she played in Christa's mental problems? She knew she hadn't been there for Christa when she needed her most. Guilt swept over the mother like a gigantic wave crashing upon the beach, pushing her under the ocean of despair she had been living in since Christa's arrest.

"Pike's history reflects impulsive self-destructive behavior in terms of drug use and sexual promiscuity, both risky activities. Things potentially threatening to self," Engum continued.

"In addition, Christa suffers from paranoid idealization. In her mind, anyone who made small talk with Tadaryl was seducing him. That's how her mind works. To Christa, they were trying to rip off her love object. She would go into incredible levels of anger and hostility toward the person she saw as a threat. Christa would become almost uncontrollable."

The jury sat in silent concentration, listening intently to every word the psychologist said. It would be their job to decide if his mental evaluation of Christa would give them any reason to find her not guilty of the heinous crime of which she was accused.

"In my opinion, she basically did not act with deliberation or premeditation, but acted in a manner consistent with her diagnosis of borderline personality disorder. She basically went out of control and lost a sense of what she was doing," Engum testified, supporting the defense's contention that Christa murdered Colleen in a fit of rage she could not control.

"When dancing afterward, she had an emotional release, a sense of relief that she'd assured, through the killing of Colleen Slemmer, her relationship with Tadaryl Shipp. The euphoria, giddiness, dancing is a reflection of that relief. Showing the bone gave her a sense of identity. Cutting the crotch of Colleen's jeans was her attempt to send a message to anyone who might be after Tadaryl," Engum stated.

There was no question that Christa had killed Colleen, or that it took thirty to sixty minutes to complete the brutal act, but Dr. Engum claimed Christa was in a frenzy. Once the attack started, it caused her to escalate and literally be out of control.

Assistant District Attorney Crabtree challenged Christa's mental disassociation. "She indicated to the police she was out of control, but remember her intelligence," Crabtree said, looking at the jury. "She said, 'I thought I heard something. I got up to go see if anyone was coming.' She took a break. She could have stopped. She removed herself from the scene, but she went back. Christa may have intended to beat Colleen, but she took a box cutter and a meat cleaver with her. She intended to kill her. Weren't these examples that Pike really acted with deliberation and premeditation?" Crabtree asked.

"I see it as a frenzy, as a complete loss of control," Engum replied.

"Is this a treatable psychological disorder?" Crabtree asked.

"Yes," Engum responded. "But, if she lied, I could change my opinion."

The last statement stuck in the minds of spectators and jurors. Was Christa telling the truth when she claimed to have gone into a fit of uncontrollable anger, or did she methodically, purposefully set out to kill Colleen Slemmer? The jury would soon be deliberating the question.

What the jury and court visitors did not hear was a statement Christa had made during one of her psychological evaluations. As a child, Christa would visit her grandfather's slaughterhouse. The youngster would pet the animals, befriend them. Then, with obvious pleasure, Christa would watch the butchery of the helpless beasts, getting a degree of sexual satisfaction from seeing them die.

The enjoyment of killing animals, or watching them be killed, is a characteristic of many serial killers, such as Ricky "Butcher" Green of Texas, Jeffrey Dahmer of Wisconsin, Bobby Long of Florida, Lawrence "Pliers" Bittaker of California, Kenneth Bianchi, the "Hillside Strangler," and Richard Ramaros of California. Evidently, Christa Pike was also exhilarated by the death of helpless beings. Armed with this information and the evaluation of Dr. Engum, another psychologist, who did not testify before the court, believed Christa fit the profile of a serial killer—only she was caught on the first kill.

Aileen Wuornos of Florida is the only female serial killer who has been arrested, therefore little is known about female serial killers. Most serial killers are male, white, and in their twenties or thirties at the time of their murders. Many of the other characteristics of multiple murderers could fit either male or female perpetrators. Most have IQ scores in the normal range, some in the superior range. (Christa's IQ was ranked at 111, slightly above average.)

Generally, serial killers' deviant behaviors were present or developing since their childhoods. They grew up in an environment in which their actions were ignored, and no limits were set. Like

Christa's mother, the parents of serial killers failed to teach their children right from wrong. They failed to learn that they live in a society that encompasses other people as well as themselves. They were never taught acceptable social interaction.

Without nurturing relationships in their early years from eight to twelve, all their negative tendencies were reinforced. They had no one to whom they could turn, and most, like Christa, grew up increasingly lonely and isolated. That isolation is an important aspect of their psychological makeup.

Finally, the unnurtured, potential murderer kills. He/she is often frightened, and at the same time thrilled. Just as Christa was frightened that someone may have seen her slaughter Colleen Slemmer, she still danced with glee at the bloody sight of her victim.

Although serial killers are most often male, neglect has many faces—even the sweet, angelic face of nineteen-year-old Christa Pike.

Yet another psychologist, who studied Christa's background, diagnosed the teen as having Mixed Personality Disorder (with Paranoid, Dependent, Borderline, Antisocial features) and Depressive Disorder.

The essential feature of Paranoid Personality Disorder is a pattern of pervasive distrust and suspicion of others. They assume that other people will exploit, harm, or deceive them, even if no evidence exists to support this expectation. They suspect that others are plotting against them and may attack them, even if little evidence exists. They feel deeply injured by another person, even when not justified. They are preoccupied with doubts about the loyalty or trustworthiness of friends and associates. Individuals with Paranoid Personality Disorder persistently bear grudges and are unwilling to forgive. Minor slights arouse major hostility. They are quick to counterattack and react with anger to perceived insults. They are pathologically jealous, and often gather circumstantial "evidence" to support their jealous beliefs. They want to maintain complete control of intimate relationships to avoid being betrayed.

Christa Pike had displayed such irrational behaviors, particularly in regard to her efforts to protect her relationship with Tadaryl Shipp—an alliance Christa refused to believe Colleen Slemmer didn't wish to destroy.

Christa Pike, like others who show features of a Dependent Personality Disorder, went to great lengths to obtain nurturance and support from others. Individuals with Dependent Personality Disorder are willing to submit to what others want, even if the demands are unreasonable. Christa, who claimed to be a Christian, a believer in God, went along with Tadaryl Shipp and his pagan rituals in order to preserve his love. That need to maintain her bond with Tadaryl resulted in an imbalanced and distorted relationship.

Like many individuals with Dependent Personality Disorder, Christa felt uncomfortable, even helpless, when alone. After leaving her mother in North Carolina for the Knoxville Job Corps, Christa had quickly attached herself to Tadaryl Shipp. Within weeks, she had become so dependent on Tadaryl that she could not see herself living without him. The threat of losing him was too much to bear.

Individuals with Dependent Personality Disorder are often characterized by pessimism and self-doubt. They tend to belittle their abilities and assets, and may constantly refer to themselves as "stupid." When Christa told Colleen Slemmer that Tadaryl could be so much more than she could ever be, she was seeing herself as worthless.

Individuals with a Borderline Personality Disorder make frantic efforts to avoid real or imagined abandonment. The feeling of impending separation or rejection can lead to significant changes in the individual's self-image and/or behavior. They experience intense abandonment fears and inappropriate anger, panic, or fury. Usually these people have a self-image that is based on being bad or evil.

Episodes of anger, panic, or despair are rarely relieved by periods of well-being or satisfaction. The episodes may reflect the individual's extreme reactivity to interpersonal stresses, just as Christa reacted to the perceived threat of losing Tadaryl. Like Christa, individuals with Borderline Personality Disorder frequently express inappropriate, intense anger, or have difficulty controlling their anger. They display extreme sarcasm, bitterness, or verbal outbursts. These episodes occur most frequently in response to a real or imagined abandonment.

Antisocial Personality Disorder is characterized by a disregard for, and violation of, the rights of others that begins in childhood and continues into adulthood. The pattern has also been referred to as "psychopathy" and "sociopathy." Deceit and manipulation are central features.

The diagnosis of Antisocial Personality Disorder is given to an individual who is at least eighteen years of age with a history of conduct disorder, which falls into four categories: aggression toward people and animals; destruction of property; deceitfulness or theft; and serious violation of rules.

Those individuals with Antisocial Personality Disorder fail to conform to social norms with respect to lawful behavior. Decisions are made on the spur of the moment, without forethought, and without consideration for the consequences to the self or others. They tend to be irritable and aggressive and may repeatedly get into physical fights or commit acts of physical assault.

They may tend to be consistently and extremely irresponsible. They show little remorse for the consequences of their acts. They may be indifferent to, or provide a superficial rationalization for, having hurt, or mistreated someone. These individuals often blame the victims for being foolish, helpless, or deserving their fate; they may minimize the harmful consequences of their actions;

or they may simply indicate complete indifference. Christa displayed these very characteristics when she blamed Colleen for the attack that ultimately took her life.

Antisocial Personality Disorder in an individual may be associated with Depressive Disorder. Episodes of Major Depressive Disorder often follow a severely stressful situation at first, but may play less of a role in subsequent episodes. Substance dependence could contribute to the onset of Major Depressive Disorder.

Regardless of the diagnosis by the various psychologists, they all agreed on one thing: Christa Pike was a very disturbed young woman.

Only one defense witness remained in Christa's trial.

Dr. William Bernet, associated with Vanderbilt University, appeared as an expert on Satanic rituals and witchcraft.

"This fits a pattern of adolescent dabbling in Satanism. A common thing. Angry children are usually involved in this type of activity. They express rage through Satanism," Bernet stated.

Dr. Bernet's statement rang true for nearly fifteen students at the Job Corps which investigating detectives found to be toying in the occult. Discovered in their search of the dorm were satanic documents, perhaps written in the victim's blood, and an altar in Tadaryl Shipp's room, along with a satanic bible and statue.

Shipp appeared to be like many young people fascinated by the occult, customizing beliefs and rituals to fit his desires and personality. Opposite from organized religion, the occult is about chaos and terror—like the killing of Colleen Slemmer.

"The statement made by Christa Pike, the autopsy, the description of what happened that night, it did not look like a Satanic ceremony or sacrifice. It appears to be collective aggression. That happens when a group of individuals are together. They become agitated and aroused and do something violent. I think it happened in this case," Bernet said.

Those people who'd sat through the entire trial remembered Christa's oral statement played by the prosecution. Christa had described how Shadolla Peterson yelled to her after she first stabbed Colleen. "You're going to prison. You have to do something," Peterson had yelled frantically. Had that been the vehicle that transported Christa from controlled anger to violent rage?

Bernet completed his testimony by stating that he negated there was any conspiracy on the part of Christa, indicating that the murder was spontaneous, rather than planned.

The defense rested. Christa's plight would soon be turned over to the jury. Talman and Martin had only one more chance to convince the twelve jurors that Christa murdered Colleen in a fit of rage, not in a planned plot. They prepared themselves for closing arguments.

Raul Martinez sat next to his wife, May, waiting

for prosecutors to present their final arguments in the case of Christa Pike. Raul gave May's hand a squeeze of encouragement. They agreed that Christa should be found guilty of the monstrous slaying of Colleen. Raul was in Knoxville to support May and to see that justice was done for the stepdaughter he had raised since she was seven. A girl he considered his own child.

As closing arguments began, Assistant District Attorney Helm reviewed more than eighty exhibits introduced by the state during the trial. While asking jurors to think about the brutal, deliberate nature of the killing, Helms held a box containing the shattered skull of Colleen Slemmer. Then she held up the blood-soaked cloth used to gag Colleen—to remind jurors that Christa had taken the cloth from her own hair to put it in Colleen's mouth in order to silence her.

Jurors glanced from the attractive assistant district attorney to Christa Pike. Christa's dark brown hair was pulled back from her face and held in place by a white strip of cloth wrapped around her naturally curly locks. The jury's gaze drifted back to the white cloth held by Helm. If jurors were envisioning Christa stripping the fabric from her hair and securing it around Colleen's mouth, the visualization could be devastating for Christa Pike.

Christa's black leather jacket, her shoes and jeans, the piece of bone from Colleen's skull, the photos of the bludgeoned, bloody body lying in a refuse pile all helped Helm reiterate to the jury the intensity, the cruelty with which Colleen Slemmer's life was extinguished.

Defense attorney William Talman did not have any inflammatory physical evidence to impress the jury with. He could tell jurors that his client only intended to beat up Slemmer. "She became involved in a fight that turned into a frenzy she could not control," Talman said.

Talman and co-counsel Julie Martin hoped that the jury would accept their explanation for the overkill, the annihilation of Colleen Slemmer by their client. But lawyers on the prosecution differed on how far they believed Christa meant to go to keep Colleen from taking her boyfriend.

" 'Colleen, do you know what's doing this to you?' " Crabtree quoted Pike from the statement she gave police regarding the moment Colleen lay on the ground, unable to speak.

"The last words she heard before she left this earth were from the mouth of the person who killed her. She had the audacity to ask the question, 'Colleen, do you know what's doing this to you?' " Crabtree said with emotion.

The courtroom was silent.

Judge Leibowitz finally broke the absolute quiet with instructions to the jury, giving them the option of convicting on lesser offenses, including reckless homicide, which Talman had urged them to consider in his closing statement.

Expressionless, the twelve jurors retired to deliberate Christa Pike's guilt or innocence on the first-degree-murder charge, in addition to a charge of conspiracy to commit murder.

Christa was taken back down to the basement of the Knoxville City-County Building to the Knox County Jail. There she would await the return of the jury's verdict, while her mother lingered in the courtroom.

Raul and May Martinez nervously waited, along with reporters and courtroom spectators, for the verdict. They were anxious for the jury to render its decision. They had anticipated this moment for over a year, each day missing their daughter as much as the day before. They hoped they wouldn't have to wait long for the jury to return with a judgment that would avenge Colleen's death.

After getting a cup of coffee from the third-floor City-County Coffee Shop, May and Raul wandered outside to the open-air rest area. The March air, chilled by a breeze that blew across the Tennessee River, cut through May.

The banks of the river, which flowed through the heart of the city, were dotted with businesses, tall trees, and docked boats. The icy waters divided the city of Knoxville. To some the river meant commerce; to others recreation. To May it was a sign of the cold, deep loss she felt.

Two and a half hours after the jury retired to deliberate, the verdict was in. Spectators took their seats. The courtroom was hushed, waiting for the jury forewoman to announce the verdict.

"Guilty." The word rang through the courtroom like a thunderous blast.

Christa turned to her mother, both women with tears in their eyes, and told her, "Don't cry." Carissa Hansen left the courtroom in silence while Raul and May embraced. They were one step closer to seeing Christa Pike pay the ultimate price for taking Colleen's life.

"I would like to see her fry," Raul said, minutes after the jury forewoman had announced the murder conviction, as well as a conviction for conspiracy to commit first-degree murder. "I'm sorry, but that's the way I feel."

For the first time since the trial began, May left the courtroom with a smile on her face.

Tears welled in the eyes of Mike Deacy, Colleen's natural father, who had traveled from Pennsylvania for the verdict.

"It's been hard to watch, hard to listen to, and I'm just glad it's over," Deacy said.

But Deacy, the Martinezes, and Christa's family would have another day of trial to endure. The penalty hearing, determining if Christa would spend the rest of her natural life in prison or be condemned to death, would be held the next morning.

It would be only the second time in Knox County history that a woman would face the threat of the death penalty. It had been ten years since Memphis had sentenced the last woman to die in the Tennessee electric chair.

Only time would tell if the Pike jury could send

young Christa to her death. Even the seasoned prosecutors had their doubts.

In seeking the death penalty, prosecutors indicated that they would rely on aggravating factors, including the crime's heinous nature. The defense would be offering mitigating circumstances, such as Christa's young age, for the jury to consider. If jurors believed the aggravating factors outweighed the mitigating circumstances, Christa Pike would be sentenced to death.

Fifteen

Christa Pike's sometimes flirtatious spirit was gone, replaced by a grave countenance as she waited for the penalty phase of her first-degree-murder conviction to begin. She and her mother exchanged soulful looks as tears filled the eyes of both.

Carissa Hansen would do anything to save Christa's life.

"May, would you change your mind and ask the prosecutors to request life in prison, rather than death for Christa?" Carissa had pleaded with the slain girl's mother.

May looked up into the sad eyes of statuesque Carissa Hansen. She, too, was an agonizing mother. A mother who could also lose her daughter to the same senseless, impetuous act to which May had lost Colleen.

"I can't," May replied with an edge of bitterness in her voice. "I just can't do that. I think it's a lot for you to ask."

May wished she could be more charitable, but in truth, she wanted Christa to die. Wanted her to pay the supreme price for taking Colleen's life. She believed that was the only fair punishment for what Christa had done. She and Raul sat hand in hand as the first witness for the defense took the stand.

Christa's aunt, Carrie Ross, began to paint a picture for the court of a very troubled young woman. A woman whose life was difficult from the day of her birth.

"Christa was premature. She was very sick and taken from her mother to another hospital for special care," Ross said. "She had no maternal bonding. Christa was four days old before her mother ever held her."

Ross had nothing positive to say about her sister, Carissa. "Christa's mom left her with her grandmother while she worked two jobs. She was rarely at home. When she wasn't working, she was out partying. Carissa needed a lot of nice clothes to go and party, so there was rarely enough money for Christa, or her younger sister, to have coats or gloves, any decent clothes. I usually took her to my house to eat," Ross said.

Her face filled with regret, Carissa Hansen sat with her head bowed. She accepted with sadness the words her sister spoke. She had not been the kind of mother Christa needed to help her grow into a responsible adult.

"Carissa neglected Christa. I would go by the house and find Christa crawling through dog poop. The house was never clean. There were dirty dishes everywhere. The house was filthy. I'd clean it," Ross testified with condemnation in her voice.

Ross related to jurors a family plagued by substance abuse, starting with her own father, an abusive addict, and her alcoholic mother.

"Mom was verbally abusive. She beat Christa and put her in a room alone for long periods of time," Ross told jurors.

Then Ross returned to her biting description of her sister as a selfish, uncaring mother.

"Carissa always came first. She and I went out to a bar one night and while we were there, we got a call from our mom. She was watching Christa. She said Christa, who was two or three at the time, was having a seizure. I told Carissa we needed to go home, but she said, 'Ah, no, it will be okay.' I made her go home and we had to take Christa to the hospital."

The jury listened closely as Carrie Ross detailed Christa's early childhood, a childhood plagued by a self-absorbed mother. There was no indication on their faces if the early life of the young woman they had just convicted of murder had any emotional effect on them and the weighty decision they would be making.

"There was no discipline, no rules in Carissa's house. Once Carissa got a letter from a man she knew out of state and she shuffled Christa off to live with her father, while she took off for North Carolina.

"After that, Delfa Pike, Christa's paternal grandmother, raised her. They were inseparable.

Mrs. Pike did everything for Christa. She fixed breakfast before she got up each morning; she took good care of her. But when Christa was eight, Mrs. Pike died. Christa was hysterical at the funeral. Her grandmother was everything to her."

Christa dabbed her eyes with a tissue as her aunt spoke of her grandmother. Grandma Pike had been Christa's world, the only stabilizing force in an otherwise scattered life. Even though it had been more than ten years since her death, Christa remembered the love, the caring.

Ross explained that after the death of Mrs. Pike, Christa's behavior changed. She went from a little girl who would sit with Ross's daughter and happily play Barbie dolls and dress-up, to an incorrigible child. She began to be uneasy about having Christa around her children. She feared for their safety.

Ross characterized Christa as a child filled with anger caused by a mother who abandoned her for a boyfriend from out of state. Then she saw her grandmother's death as yet another abandonment. A painful parting.

But the witness's attempt to explain why Christa harbored internal hostility was exploited on cross-examination. The prosecution focused on the destructive side of Christa's personality.

"You said you were afraid to have Christa around your kids, is that correct?" Crabtree asked.

The witness reluctantly answered, "Yes."

"You said she was out of control since she was

eight, that her mother couldn't control her, and that she didn't go to school. And out of all the family difficulties, Christa is the only one who's murdered, isn't that right?" Crabtree drilled the witness.

"Yes," Ross responded softly.

As Ross left the stand, she smiled at Christa. She had done all she could to help her niece. Now it was Christa's father's turn to try to save his daughter's life.

Emil Glenn Pike had been married to Christa's mother twice. He told the court that during their first marriage, his and Christa's relationship was good, but during his second marriage to Carissa, he hadn't been around much. After the couple's second divorce, Emil remarried and maintained a long-distance relationship with his daughter.

Emil explained that there were periods of time when Christa's mother, unable to control her daughter, would send her to live with him. Christa's life at her father's home was filled with turmoil as well. She performed badly in school, she and her stepmother did not get along, and Christa was jealous of her father's new family. During one of Christa's fits of jealousy, an incident occurred with Emil's youngest daughter.

Although Christa denied the allegation, she had been accused of sexually abusing her two-year-old half-sister. Angry with Christa, Emil had sent her back to Carissa. Again she felt abandoned. Christa believed her father had chosen his new wife and family over her. It was another painful severance for Christa.

"I didn't know her mother was allowing her to run the streets at all hours of the day and night. I know that her mother drank and smoked pot," Emil told jurors.

Then Emil told the jury that just before Christa's eighteenth birthday she asked him to sign papers for her to be adopted. "She didn't want my name," Emil said, with a tone of sadness.

Members of the media wondered if Christa's request hadn't been a cry for attention, a cry for help from her father. After all, at seventeen, Christa had already established a pattern of defiance. Who would adopt a teenager so obviously troubled?

Although Emil Pike loved his daughter, he had truthfully characterized Christa as a troubled teen who was a liar and a manipulator.

Christa watched her father leave the witness stand. She managed a slight smile for him, realizing that his testimony had been difficult.

Carissa Hansen took a deep breath, gave her daughter a quick grin, and headed to the witness chair. She had endured the testimonies of both her sister and ex-husband. They had characterized her as a horrible mother. Carissa had to agree. She had never been there for Christa. She could rectify some of the damage by doing all she could to help her daughter live.

Christa's mother began by explaining that she and Emil Pike had divorced because he did not work, while she was holding down two jobs. They remarried after he obtained employment, but after he quit, she was back to two jobs a day, leaving little time for Christa.

In 1983, Carissa married Danny Thompson of North Carolina. "Danny and Christa didn't get along," Carissa explained. "I left Christa with her grandmother and her dad. Danny had said, 'It's Christa or me.'"

When Carissa had chosen Danny, Christa's feelings of abandonment had escalated.

"In 1988, Grandma Pike died of cancer. Christa had wanted to stay home with Grandma and take care of her. She felt like she was the caretaker. Christa was only eight, so her father sent her to me. Christa felt that because she didn't stay and care for Grandma Pike, she died. She cried for days. She didn't go to school. She ran away. Not long after the funeral, Christa overdosed."

Christa pressed a clean white tissue to her eyes. May Martinez sat expressionless as she watched Christa wipe away tears. Indeed, Christa's life had been filled with turmoil, but was that a reason to kill? May shook her head.

"The principal called me from school and told me to take her to a psychiatrist. She admitted taking pills. Except for the day of the overdose, Christa received no further treatment for her depression.

"When Christa came to live with me, she was home alone a lot. Christa was shuttled back and forth between her dad and me. There'd be relationship problems so, for a break, I'd send her to her dad. After a while, he'd send her back to me," Carissa said.

During this period of unrest, Christa not only failed to establish a permanent relationship with either parent, but was faced with continually having to make new friends in different schools. Again and again, Christa's feelings of abandonment were bolstered.

Carissa told the court that in 1989 she had a relationship with Steve Kyaw. Christa didn't like him; he often beat her with a belt. Deciding not to take the punishment any longer, Christa threatened him with a butcher knife. At age twelve, Christa was reeling further out of control.

"I was not there for her. I should be the one in her seat, not her," Carissa said with tears running down her cheeks. "I should be the one to be punished for this crime, not her. I was a terrible mother."

Christa watched as her mother wiped the tears from her face. Christa sobbed. Both mother and daughter felt the pain of the lost years.

May Martinez was astonished. How could Christa's family ignore her while she was growing up, and then, when something like this happened, show such concern and try to stop an execution?

"I had no control over Christa. No one did. She pretty much did what she wanted to. She would run away. The police would bring her home. She would run away again. She didn't want to be in my house," Carissa said sadly.

"What did you do?" Talman asked.

"Nothing. I drank. I felt sorry for myself."

"She had live-in boyfriends, what, when she was fourteen years old?" Talman inquired.

"She had a live-in boyfriend. I let him move in because she was so infatuated with him. I was afraid she would leave again and be living on the streets. So, rather than them live on the streets, I let him live with me," Carissa answered.

"She was growing marijuana in the house at nine years old?" the defense prodded.

"Oh, I think she was older than that," Carissa said, apparently trying to minimize the infraction.

"She had been institutionalized for a period of time on a couple of occasions?" Talman asked.

"That's correct. She did well while she was there. But when she got out, she just went back to the same old friends. She always followed what her friends wanted," Carissa stated.

Both prosecutors scribbled on the yellow legal pads in front of them, preparing for cross-examination.

Carissa told the jury that when Christa was at the Job Corps, she brought her mother to the dorm for a visit. Carissa described walls with CRYPTS RULE and GANG DISCIPLES scrawled on them. Gang colors of blue and red were smeared across the walls. There was blood all over the doorway of the men's room, trailing down the hall. It was a depiction of a place as out of control as her daughter.

The prosecution ignored the Job Corps problems, and concentrated on Christa herself. Crabtree emphasized Christa's potentially violent behavior when she threatened her mom's boyfriend with the butcher knife. Under cross-examination, Carissa also admitted that her daughter, at age twelve, began carrying a knife in her purse.

When questioned about Christa's entrance into the Job Corps, the defendant's mother denied her daughter was sent to the Job Corps after an incident where she and her friends kicked in the door of someone's house.

"That had nothing to do with it," Carissa protested. "She had already planned to go to the Job Corps." But the question had raised the possibility of other unlawful acts committed by Christa.

Crabtree persisted until Carissa admitted that Christa had been a habitual runaway, that she'd lied, stolen, that she'd been given a number of second chances, but had blown all of them. With her mother's testimony, Crabtree managed to portray Christa as a troubled youth who was beyond help.

Christa Pike's deviant behavior was typical of other adolescents convicted of homicide. Christa came from a home with poor supervision by parents, an absent father figure, an emotionally cold mother, a sense of abandonment and distrust, and a family marked by turmoil. It was these circumstances the defense hoped would sway the jury to leniency for their client.

The prosecution, on the other hand, hoped the jury found Christa to be self-focused and manipulative. A person who would go after what she wanted with little or no guilt. Christa's diagnosis of Borderline Personality Disorder was akin to Antisocial Personality. She displayed many of the marks of a psychopath: superficial charm, and average or better intelligence; chronic lying; inability to feel guilt or shame; poor judgment and inability to learn from her experiences; lack of empathy; impulse preferred over deliberation; and, as a child, truancy, vandalism, lying, fighting, stealing, and persistent breaking of home rules.

In rebuttal to the defense, Crabtree called just one witness, the University of Tennessee Officer Harold Underwood. Crabtree questioned Underwood about the day he was positioned at the crime scene to protect it from intruders.

"She seemed amused. She was giggling and moving around," Underwood described his conversation with Christa the day Colleen's body was discovered.

The prosecution's firm belief that Christa Pike would be a continued threat to society propelled them to seek the death penalty.

"Ladies and gentlemen of the jury," Assistant District Attorney Helms began her summation. "I am going to be brief. General Crabtree has told you that the state is relying on two aggravating circumstances in asking you to consider the death penalty in this case. Those two facts are that the murder was especially heinous, and it involved torture or serious physical abuse beyond that necessary to produce death. And the murder was committed for the purpose of avoiding, interfering with, or preventing a lawful arrest or prosecution of the defendant herself, or someone else.

"In your deliberations yesterday, you considered all of the proof that had been presented in the matter. You have the evidence at your disposal, but I'm going to ask you to look at this exhibit introduced by Dr. Elkins," Helm said, pointing to a chart depicting the numerous wounds on the body of Colleen Slemmer.

"You will recall that Dr. Elkins testified that she stopped counting all the major wounds at the letter 'W' after starting with the letter 'A'. She put this letter here to indicate the innumerable other superficial slash wounds on the back, arms, and chest of the victim," Helms said, again pointing to the chart.

"You will also recall that she testified that all the slash, cut, stab, and laceration wounds suffered by this victim occurred before her death from the crushing of her skull. I suggest to you that any definition of heinous or cruel is screaming from this chart right now. There is no doubt that Colleen Slemmer was tortured. It was cruel. It was heinous, vile.

"There is another one of Dr. Elkins's exhibits that only goes to amplify the aggravating factor I've been talking about. You've seen this," Helms acknowledged as she held up a diagram of Colleen's mutilated skull.

"And you have seen the pictures represented by this very antiseptic diagram. You know from the testimony of witnesses that her face was virtually unrecognizable. And I suggest to you that this picture falls within any definition of heinous or cruel.

"As to the second aggravating factor, the defendant herself told you, 'When I realized I was going to get arrested, I thought, I can't let Colleen go. She can't leave this place.' She killed her to keep herself out of trouble. That aggravating factor, along with the first has been proven to you beyond a reasonable doubt, which is the standard the state is held to.

"The state will ask you to act on everything you've seen in this courtroom the last six days and to return a judgment of death. Thank you."

The courtroom was silent. Only the sound of Helms's footsteps broke the silence as she returned to the prosecutors' table. She could only wait while the defense presented their closing arguments, then listen to Crabtree reiterate the state's desire to see Christa Pike be sentenced to death.

May and Raul Martinez patiently waited through closing remarks for the time when Judge Leibowitz would charge the jury with the task of sentencing Colleen's murderer. They only hoped the seven men and five women would have the courage to take the life of the person who had killed their daughter.

On the opposite side of the courtroom, Carissa Hansen nervously twisted a tissue in her hands. She tried to smile when Christa turned to look at her. Then their attention turned to Julie Martin, who stood before the jury.

"Ladies and gentlemen, Christa Gail Pike sits here convicted of murder in the first degree for an act that was committed when she was eighteen years old. A young girl who never got out of the starting gate of life. How do you convey a lifetime of rejection and abuse in an hour or so? You can't. But you can get the picture. An idea."

Martin's long, brown hair swung slightly as she paced the floor.

"Christa's aunt, Carrie Ross, has told you what her life was like. She was left in the care of other people. Carrie saw her own mother, an alcoholic, scream at Christa for the littlest thing. Spank her for the smallest things. She kept Christa. Why? Because her mother had to go back to work two weeks after she was born. She was working two jobs sometimes. Her mother wasn't there.

"Then Christa was left with a paternal grandmother. She adored Grandma Pike and Grandma Pike adored her. Christa did everything with her. She loved her. Grandma Pike took care of Christa—and then she died. That little girl"—Martin pointed to Christa as she addressed the jury—"was devastated, hysterical over that death."

Christa's expression was one of sadness. But was she saddened by the memory of her dear grandmother, or at the possibility of facing death herself? The jurors were uncertain. Was Christa Pike a victim, as the defense contended, or was she the psychopathic killer portrayed by the prosecution? The jurors gave no indication from their blank expressions what they believed.

"When Christa was twelve, things were getting out of hand. You heard of truancy, runaway, living on the streets. And what was happening to Christa? Mom's over here partying. Mom's choosing boyfriends over her own daughter. Where is Christa? Send her off to Dad. Her father could not be concerned enough to find out all this stuff that was going on. He told you that. He didn't know she was in all that trouble. He didn't know how bad it was. Is that a concerned father? When he had trouble with her, he sent her back to Mom. Another rejection by her father was an allegation of something. He chose, ladies and gentlemen, his new wife, his new family over Christa. When she called to go back to him, he told her, 'No, you can't come back here.' And the last rejection, insult, injury, was that he was going to sign his rights away, give her up for adoption.

"Carissa Hansen, Christa's mother, got up on the stand and told you, 'I'm a terrible mother.' She admits it. She admits she didn't do what she should have done for Christa when these problems arose. She took her to treatment a couple of times, but there was no follow through, no discipline. In the meantime, Christa is getting bounced back and forth. She is going to a father who enforces the rules to a mother who wants to be her friend—smokes pot with her. She's an alcoholic. She lets boys live with Christa. Who is giving Christa direction? Who is enforcing rules? What kind of message is being sent to Christa that she was a worthwhile individual? That she was loved? I suggest to you that there is not a message that she is loved. I suggest to you, she was not worthwhile. 'You are causing problems, Christa, go away. I can't deal with you, go away. I have a life to lead. I want this man over you.'

"Her father is not involved, out of touch. Her mother is into herself and all she had was an aunt that tried to do what she could. Carrie Ross would go to the house, clean up the dog stools that Christa was crawling through. Because Christa's mother can't be concerned with that, she is too busy partying. Her mother is too busy with her own self, her own life. The pattern is repeated over and over. Increasing problems. The one person she loved is gone. Nobody loves her. She is living on the streets. Who is going to want her now? She wants that attention, that self-esteem. I suggest that was what was going through her mind—even if not consciously." Martin was clearly emotional.

May Martinez stared at Christa Pike. She couldn't see the child Martin described, only a cold-blooded, remorseless killer.

"You may consider all you've heard through

the guilty and penalty phases. What you have seen and heard is a picture of someone struggling to find out who she is and to find some reason to be alive and be worthwhile. Ladies and gentlemen, I would suggest that Christa Pike is the poster child for the result of breakdown in family values. Exactly what the moral majority is fighting to prevent."

Martin's reference to the moral majority was a direct hit at jurors who resided in this southern Bible-belt state.

"I suggest that any aggravated circumstances do not outweigh the mitigating circumstances of this case. I would suggest to you, do not kill Christa Gail Pike. Choose life. Thank you."

The passionate closing remarks of Julie Martin could be felt in the courtroom as if they were a thick fog wrapping each person within its mist. Soft sobs could be heard from both Christa and her mother. Emil Pike's head drooped in what some spectators believed was shame. Indeed, Christa Pike had lived a life filled with many disappointments, but was it enough to spare her life?

May and Raul watched Christa and her mother exchange heartfelt glances. Bitterness filled May's own heart. Christa may have had a lot of family problems, but that was no excuse for murder. Lots of kids come from broken homes. They had problems, but they didn't commit murder. May had no sympathy for Christa Pike. Her heart hurt too badly to feel sorry for the person who'd killed Colleen.

Assistant District Attorney Crabtree approached the jury. An imposing figure, he spoke directly to the twelve people who would be making the final decision as to Christa Pike's fate.

"Ladies and gentlemen, in a case such as this there are no winners, only losers. And there is no happiness, only sadness. No one likes what has to be done in a case such as this.

"Ms. Martin has talked about the family of Christa Gail Pike and insists that she is the creation of this family. She may well be, but that's not what we are here to deal with. If this is a monster that they have created, it is a monster that we have to deal with. These same people who are telling you these things that occurred, are the father who was not willing to have her around his children, but he turns her out with our children. The aunt who was not willing to have Christa around her children, but she turned her out with our children. And the mother who was not willing to have her around her boyfriend, but turned her out with us. Ms. Martin says Christa Gail Pike was seeking a reason to live. Surely, she is not saying that Christa seeking a reason to live is the reason she killed Colleen Slemmer. There has been no proof at all in this case that says that she didn't know what she was doing. She knew what she was doing. She had planned this. She committed this offense.

"Just because Christa comes from a dysfunctional family does not mean that she should not be held responsible for her acts. According to them, this is the only family member who has murdered. The fact that her mother did not properly take care of her is not an excuse for what she did to Colleen Slemmer," Crabtree told the jury.

Pushing her blond bangs back from her face, May Martinez nodded her head in agreement. No amount of neglect could justify the torturous killing of her daughter.

"If you find that the state has not proven a statutory aggravated circumstance beyond a reasonable doubt, then it is your duty to set a punishment of life in prison. If you find that we have proven one or more statutory aggravated circumstances beyond a reasonable doubt, but that these do not outweigh any mitigating circumstances beyond a reasonable doubt, then it is your duty to make a determination as to life and life without parole. If you find that we have proven one or more aggravated circumstances beyond a reasonable doubt and that these outweigh any mitigating circumstances beyond a reasonable doubt, then it is your duty, and no one has ever indicated that you should like to have to make such a decision, but it is your duty to do what the law requires. It is your duty to return a punishment of death.

"Again, I want to emphasis that this is not what anyone likes. This is not anything that makes anyone happy, but it is something that needs to be done.

"Remember at the beginning we talked about

that what you were going to hear was going to be worse than any movie or anything you had ever read. Worse than any nightmare. That is what this case has proved to be," Crabtree said.

Raul hugged May's shoulders. Life since Colleen's murder *had* been a nightmare.

"This whole argument we've been talking here has not taken an hour, but that is the time Colleen Slemmer was being cut and slashed and beaten by cruel means to cause pain. What can you say, except that Christa intended to cause pain and torture. It was intended infliction of severe physical and mental pain upon the victim while she remained alive. Each of you can think about pain from a small wound. Even when you cut your finger with a paper cut, it hurts. Think about the cuts and slices and stab wounds that Colleen Slemmer had over her entire body and then, while she is alive and conscious, to have this pentagram carved in her chest. Is that not torture? Can you think of anything more torturous than that?

"What group of mitigating factors can outweigh this hour of pain and torture? 'Why are you doing this to me? Why are you doing this to me?' Colleen asked. And to think that this murder was committed to avoid prosecution, if you'll recall the defendant's statement. After she had cut Colleen Slemmer across the stomach, she had to kill her. She couldn't let her live. There is no question that this aggravating factor applies.

"Against this, you'll consider that this defendant has no significant history of criminal activity, that the murder was committed when the defendant was under extreme emotional disturbance, and that the youth of the defendant at the time of the crime, the capacity of the defendant to appreciate the wrongness of her conduct or to condone her conduct, were substantially impaired as a result of a mental disease or defect or intoxication. This was a list given you, but you don't have to find them just. As you don't have to find the aggravating factors. But the ones you do find, you weigh. The weight depends on the gravity of the factor and how it applies to this case." Crabtree paced in front of the railed jury box.

"If we only had the torture, that would be enough to outweigh any mitigating factor beyond a reasonable doubt. Here we have proof of two factors.

"Ladies and gentlemen, you have a duty. A duty to consider fairly all the proof. You have taken an oath to perform a duty. We think that if you follow that duty, you will find the state has carried its burden in this case. Thank you," Crabtree concluded.

There was nothing more to be said. The attorneys on both sides of the case sat silent at their respective tables. Christa Pike's fate lay in the hands of the jury.

Pushing her glasses up on the bridge of her nose, Judge Leibowitz addressed the jury. The judge restated both the aggravated and mitigating circumstances of the case. When finished, the judge gave one final instruction to the jury.

"You will write your verdict on the enclosed form," Judge Leibowitz directed as she dismissed the jury to deliberate.

The five women and seven men filed out of the courtroom. Their faces expressionless like blank canvases yet to be painted.

May Martinez looked at her watch. It was 3:05 P.M. The anxiety she felt waiting in the courtroom for the jury to return was familiar. She'd had the same gnawing feeling in the pit of her stomach when the jury had retired to deliberate guilt or innocence.

Carissa Hansen visited with Charley Belcher, telling him that she and her family wanted to thank the Knox County Sheriff's Department, court bailiffs, and the citizens of Knoxville who had recognized her during her visits as she prepared for her daughter's trial.

"I want them to know that everyone in Christa's family appreciates them," Carissa said.

At 4:30 P.M. the jury returned, only a little more than an hour after they had retired and in less time than the guilty verdict had taken.

Twenty-year-old Christa Pike began sobbing loudly and uncontrollably when Judge Leibowitz announced she would die by electrocution on January 12, 1997 for the killing of nineteen-year-old Colleen Slemmer. Ironically, that would be the second anniversary of the murder.

The state had proven that Christa had killed in

order to keep Tadaryl Shipp, the man she loved. With her death sentence, he became a love to die for.

Carissa Hansen sat sobbing behind her daughter in the courtroom.

Christa clutched a tissue to her mouth. Tears streamed down her face and she continued to sob as the judge spoke.

"May God have mercy upon you," Leibowitz said in an unshaken voice. This was Leibowitz's first death sentence. The veteran judge gave no indication that handing down the punishment was anything out of the ordinary, although the sentencing of Christa Pike distinguished the teenager as only the second woman sentenced to Tennessee's death row, and the youngest woman sentenced to die in the United States.

"Can I please hug my mom before I go? Please let me just hug my mom," Christa begged Leibowitz tearfully.

The court bailiff took Christa by the arm and led her from the courtroom to the dock, just outside the door.

"I love you," Christa said to her mother as she walked from the courtroom.

"I love you, too," Carissa responded.

Before the door to the corridor closed behind her, Christa could be heard by spectators within earshot saying, "Oh, shit," in a clear, unemotional voice. But once Christa was placed in a holding cell just off the courtroom, she could be heard crying.

Moments after the courtroom was cleared, Leibowitz allowed mother and daughter to meet before Christa was taken back to the Knox County Jail. They embraced and Carissa kissed her daughter good-bye. It was a tearful parting.

Christa's death sentence was bittersweet for May and Raul. The verdict was just, but they knew taking Christa's life would not bring Colleen back. The couple thanked the prosecutors for their diligence in trying the case, then quietly left the Knox County building.

May didn't plan to return for the trials of Shadolla Peterson and Tadaryl Shipp. "I can't relive the whole thing again," she said.

May had confidence in Knox County prosecutors to secure convictions for the two remaining defendants. She knew Crabtree and Helms would make certain that, regardless of their family backgrounds, jurors would know that Shadolla and Tadaryl, like Christa, were not the victims.

The innocent victim had been her daughter, Colleen.

Sixteen

Once her death sentence was rendered, Christa Pike returned to her familiar Knox County Jail cell. Her initial shock at the judgment soon turned to rage. She sat on the small single bunk and wrote to Tadaryl, who awaited his own trial in another section of the jail. Jail authorities intercepted the unsealed letter and turned it over to the prosecutors' office.

The letter read: "Ya see what I get for tryin' to be nice to the hoe [*sic*]. I went ahead and bashed her brains out so she'd die quickly instead of letting her bleed to death and suffer more, and they fuckin' FRY me!!! Ain't dat some shit?

"I have ten mons. [*sic*] left to live! Imagine that!" Christa told Tadaryl in the letter. "I'd spend every moment with you if I could!"

Christa, who tried to protect Tadaryl from the beginning, instructed him to change his story concerning his role in the brutal murder. She urged him to adopt her version of the events.

"Also, tell your lawyer if he wants me to testify for you . . . I WILL!" she wrote.

In closing, Christa told Tadaryl, "Love you for the rest of my life!" She signed it, "Litl Devil."

Christa gave the letter to a jailer to be passed on to her boyfriend. As far as she knew, Tadaryl had received the letter and her offer to help him during his own upcoming trial.

Christa was transferred to the Tennessee Prison for Women in Nashville, more than a hundred miles from the man she loved enough to kill for.

"I think she's an evil person," May told reporters by phone from her Orange Park, Florida, home. "I think there's something definitely messed up with her that she can go out and deliberately murder somebody."

May had been home for over a week, but the trauma of sitting in the courtroom, watching her daughter's clothing and skull presented as evidence still haunted her.

"I think they should kill her right away," May said. "That's how I feel. The taxpayers' money is paying to let her stay alive. That's terrible."

May's anger, a natural part of the grieving process, was not directed only toward Christa, Tadaryl, and Shadolla. May also held responsible Career Systems Development Corporation, which operated Job Corps, the defunct vocational and educational center for disadvantaged young people for the federal government. She believed that Career Systems was negligent in operating the center and believed they should pay for their laxness. May decided to sue Career Systems.

***

About two weeks after Christa's conviction, Shadolla Peterson appeared before Judge Leibowitz. Her hair was neatly braided on each side and tightly tied at the nape of her neck with a white band. The nineteen-year-old was neatly dressed. Cluster earrings adorned her ears.

Shadolla Peterson remained the mystery figure of the Job Corps murder. No one knew for sure what her involvement in the killing had been. But in an agreement that had been discussed for weeks before Pike's conviction, Shadolla was in court to plead guilty to accessory after the first-degree murder of Colleen Slemmer. Her attorney, District Public Defender Mark Stephens, told the court his client admitted to being present at the killing, but insisted that she did not know Slemmer was going to be murdered. "Shadolla denies taking part in the attack in any way," Stephens said.

"We think that if the case were presented to a jury, this accessory charge is what the jury would have been able to convict her on, based on available proof," Assistant District Attorney Crabtree said following the hearing.

Crabtree's co-counsel in the Pike case, Jo Helm, agreed, adding that if Peterson's case had gone to trial, the state would have offered proof that Peterson was present at the murder. Prosecutors had no other proof to tie her to the slaying. The accessory charge was the best they could do in obtaining any punishment for Peterson's role.

In exchange for her plea agreement, Peterson received credit for four hundred and sixty days in jail and was ordered to spend the balance of a six-year sentence on probation.

No one could tell from the stoic expression on Judge Leibowitz's face if she agreed with the plea bargain or if she felt Shadolla Peterson's responsibility in the murder went beyond the accessory charge. The discerning judge rendered the sentence agreed upon by the state and the defense without additional comment.

Although her expression remained pensive, Shadolla Peterson was relieved to be free from the Knox County Jail. For more than a year she had wondered if confinement was to be a way of life for years to come. She looked forward to walking out in the fresh spring air, breathing in the sweet smell of freedom. Shadolla's sad brown eyes were filled with relief, as well as sadness. She would be forever altered by the horrors that she had seen on that isolated stretch of roadway behind the UT steam plant.

Shadolla quickly fled the City-County Building without speaking to reporters.

But as happy as Shadolla was to be free, happy to be returning to her hometown of Cleveland, Tennessee, May Martinez was furious.

"I'm very, very angry about it. I think the state should ask the parents what they should do," May said, blasting prosecutors to reporters by phone following the hearing. "I think if they had a trial or some kind of thing with a judge and jury, she probably would have gotten more."

May was convinced, even if prosecutors were not, that Shadolla was more involved than she had indicated. May believed that Shadolla was dangerous. She didn't want to see her go free.

Charley Belcher agreed. "Shadolla Peterson is the luckiest girl in Tennessee," he later commented.

Crabtree and Helm understood May's anger, but they were satisfied that they had made the correct decision concerning the prosecution of Shadolla Peterson. Both skilled prosecutors believed that stronger charges than accessory after the murder wouldn't bring any stricter penalty. The evidence was not on their side—nor was time. They had to prepare for the first-degree-murder trial of Tadaryl Shipp.

Because Shipp was a juvenile at the time of the murder, Tennessee state law prohibited prosecutors from seeking the death penalty. The seventeen-year-old had dodged death, but could face life in prison for his part in the murder of Colleen Slemmer.

In a pretrial hearing, Shipp's attorney, Chris Coffey, argued that his client had been arrested wrongfully.

"The police had probable cause to arrest Shipp without a warrant because a tipster told Investigator York that Pike and Shipp were getting ready to leave town," Judge Leibowitz said in response to Coffey's motion.

"Neither Shipp nor Pike had a car, Your Honor," Coffee argued.

"That's not the only way one could leave," Leibowitz said. "One could get on a bus or hitch a ride."

Tadaryl Shipp would stand trial in Knoxville for the first-degree murder of Colleen Slemmer.

Nearly three months had passed since the conviction of Christa Pike for the murder of Colleen Slemmer. The talk of the town of Knoxville continued to be Christa Pike and the most horrible crime Knoxville had seen in years. As Charley Belcher had predicted during Tadaryl's pretrial hearing, the story was huge. He decided to make the one-hundred-mile trip west to Nashville and interview Christa at the state's women's prison.

Charley and Christa had connected during her trial. Christa had worried about her mother being in Knoxville for the trial, had worried about the treatment she would receive from the public and the press. But Charley had been polite to her mother.

"Where's a good place to eat?" Carissa Hanson had asked Belcher after one of his initial interviews. Belcher had cordially directed Carissa to a favorite local dining spot. Carissa, appreciative of the young reporter's kindness, had conveyed to Christa Charley's kindness.

Christa sat in her county jail cell and watched the television reports featuring Belcher. The tall, dark-haired, handsome reporter with deep brown eyes captivated Christa's attention. The immature young killer was attracted to the twenty-something Belcher and had made no effort to suppress her attraction in court.

Charley Belcher and his cameraman sat in a room just off the dining hall of the prison, waiting for Christa's arrival. Belcher was taken aback when the young, innocent-looking Christa Pike shuffled into the room. Steel shackles bound her ankles, and were attached to chains that encircled her waist, leading to handcuffs around her wrists. She looked harmless, nonthreatening. Their brown eyes met. In an instant, Belcher recognized he was not there to interview a helpless little girl, but a cold, callous killer. Christa sat across from Charley. The guards took no action to remove her bindings.

"Hey, how are you?" Christa asked, her voice heavy with her Southern accent.

She may look like she couldn't hurt a flea, but she's a psychotic killer, Belcher reminded himself.

"How are you doing? What is prison like for you?" Belcher asked.

"I have no problem with it," Christa said, blinking her eyes at Belcher. "I have a CD player, a TV, and VCR. I have a friend across the hall. It's not too bad."

After the initial small talk, Belcher was ready to begin. "Let's go," he instructed the cameraman.

The minute the red light flashed on the top of the video camera, indicating that tape was rolling, Christa's demeanor changed. Her flirtatious, bubbly disposition changed to a sorrowful, repentant one.

"I can't believe this happened," Christa said, sorrow dripping from her words.

"Some people think of you as a monster. What do you think?" Belcher asked.

Christa looked into the camera, expressing her regret, but her eyes gave her away. Although her words spoke of sorrow and regret, her eyes couldn't hide the piercing look of a cold-blooded killer.

"I think of Colleen often," she said. "I feel so bad."

Belcher quickly jotted down thoughts as Christa addressed his questions. He noted that Christa only spoke of her feelings, not those of her victim. She wanted his audience to know how bad *she* felt, how bad the killing had made *her* feel, and how sorry his audience should feel for her because *she* had to think about the murder every day. Christa Pike obviously thought only of herself.

But there were no tears. No outward signs of remorse or sorrow. Not until Belcher asked about Tadaryl did Christa Pike's eyes fill with tears. Her real sense of sorrow and loss was for Tadaryl, the man she would die for, not her victim.

As the interview wound down and Belcher prepared to leave, Christa had one request.

"Will you give me a hug?" she asked, the innocence back in her Southern voice.

"Sure," Belcher said hesitantly.

The reporter and the killer embraced. A shiver of regret ran down Belcher's body. He felt betrayal, disloyalty to May Martinez. He quickly backed off from Christa, thanked her for the interview and headed for the door.

Within days after the interview ran on Knoxville television, Christa Pike was back in the stern judge's court for sentencing on a charge of conspiracy to commit murder. Gone were the schoolgirl dresses with big white collars. Christa appeared in her prison blues. There would be no jury to try to persuade. This time Christa would be sentenced by Judge Leibowitz herself.

In a surprise move, William Crabtree produced the letter written by Christa to Tadaryl the day the jury announced she would die for Colleen's murder. Defense attorney William Talman was visibly shaken by the letter.

"Oh shit," Talman said under his breath as spectators gasped at the remarks written by Christa.

The stark Judge Leibowitz was noticeably irritated by Christa's harsh words and her obvious lack of regret when she wrote, "I went ahead and bashed her brains out so she'd die quickly instead of letting her bleed to death and suffer more, and they fuckin' FRY me!!!"

"I'm convinced you care about no one but yourself," Judge Leibowitz said harshly.

Christa was sentenced to a twenty-five-year prison sentence for conspiracy to commit murder. The sentence would be served consecutive to the death sentence. In addition, Christa was barred from profiting from the sale of any account of the case.

The letter, which was read in open court, shocked May and Raul Martinez, who attended the Knoxville hearing. "She has no remorse at all," May told reporters.

Raul had stronger words for the young killer. His eyes narrowed and his chin became rigid as he spoke outside the courtroom. "I don't think there's a human being inside that body," Raul commented.

As Christa left the courthouse, she smiled sweetly and gave a little closed-finger wave to Charley Belcher. Christa seemed happy, once again being the center of attention.

Seventeen

It had been a year since the conviction of Christa Pike. A year since May Martinez had sat in the small Knox County courtroom and watched her daughter's murder replayed again and again through testimony. May had no plans to attend Tadaryl's trial. She couldn't go through the emotional turbulence again.

Speculation was high that Christa Pike would be transported from the state prison in Nashville to Knoxville in order to testify on behalf of Tadaryl. Even though William Talman, Christa's attorney, advised her against appearing, Knoxville residents vividly remembered reading excerpts from Christa's letter to Tadaryl, where she had offered to testify for him.

Tadaryl Shipp entered Judge Leibowitz's court looking radically unlike the photo published in the *Knoxville News-Sentinel* following his arrest. His hair was neatly cropped close to his head, his mustache nicely trimmed. He wore a white shirt and tie. Tadaryl scarcely resembled the disorderly teen arrested two years earlier for murder.

Assistant District Attorney Crabtree repeated his key points of the case during opening statements; many details duplicated those spoken during the Pike trial. He told the Shipp panel, just as he had the Pike jury, that the murder "was as bad or worse than your worst nightmare."

Tadaryl sat stone faced beside his attorneys. His lack of expression gave no indication of regret.

"When she tried to run away, Shipp chased her and brought her back," Crabtree said. "And then, after Colleen Slemmer was dead, he took one foot and Christa Pike took the other foot, and they dragged her up on this pile of rubble."

Crabtree ended his opening remarks by telling the jury, "You are going to hear about the tragic, the cruel, and totally unnecessary killing of Colleen Slemmer."

Tadaryl's mother sat behind her only child as the prosecution accused him of murder. Her face revealed the same pain that had been seen in Christa Pike's mother's face a year earlier.

Defense attorney Coffey took the floor and walked to the jurors' box.

"There is one person in this case that had a motive," Coffey said. "And her name was Christa Pike."

It was immediately obvious to everyone in the courtroom that Tadaryl Shipp's defense was to place blame, all the blame, squarely on the shoulders of Christa Pike.

"There will be no proof that Tadaryl Shipp had any motive," Coffey stated.

"Pike and Peterson were participating in gathering weapons. Tadaryl Shipp didn't do it. He didn't do that. You won't hear proof that he did.

"But on the evening in question, those two people had a plan. They wanted to scare Colleen. They wanted to hurt her. They wanted to do something. Mr. Shipp finds out about it. He says, 'Well, I'm going to go, too.' He shouldn't have gone. He had no motive to do it. But he went.

"Maybe he thought, as a teenager, 'There's some girls that like me, boy, this will be interesting.' He didn't know what was going to happen. There isn't any proof that he planned on doing it," Coffey said.

Tadaryl's mother dabbed her eyes with a hanky.

"In a moment up there that night one person made a decision to kill," Coffey passionately told jurors. "That one person was Christa Pike, the one that got the weapons, the one that had the motive, the one that didn't like her.

"Tadaryl didn't have any business being up there, he didn't have any reason to be up there. When Christa killed her, he had walked away. He didn't want to see that."

As Coffey explained to jurors that Tadaryl had cut Colleen, but that the wounds were not severe enough to cause unconsciousness, much less death, reporters who had covered the Pike trial shuddered. From the photos, diagrams, and physical evidence presented during the Pike trial, there was nothing insignificant about any of the wounds suffered by Colleen Slemmer.

"Christa Pike decided to kill her. It was not a conspiracy. Tadaryl didn't intend for that to happen. He didn't join with Christa in her intent. Shadolla Peterson didn't decide to kill her. Tadaryl Shipp didn't decide to kill her. What they did was criminal, but it is not first-degree murder. They didn't conspire.

"You can find Tadaryl Shipp guilty of criminal action, but he is not guilty of first-degree murder. He is not guilty of conspiracy to commit first-degree murder.

"One person is guilty of murder. And that person is Christa Pike. Thank you," Coffey concluded.

After the court took a ten-minute recess to bring in exhibits, the trial of Tadaryl Shipp progressed in the much the same form and manner as that of Christa Pike. The prosecution began with Duncan Sutherland, University of Tennessee groundskeeper. Then Officer John Johnson described a crime scene that depicted an intense struggle that covered several yards. The second day of court, Dr. Sandra Elkins took the stand.

This was the second jury to hear about the gruesome, anguished slaying of Colleen Slemmer. Unlike Christa's trial, the prosecution elected not to enter the skull of Colleen Slemmer into evidence. Instead, Crabtree and Helm opted to use graphic photographs and diagrams, while having Drs. Elkins and Marks describe the multiple wounds of the victim.

Beginning with his opening statement and

throughout the court proceedings, defense attorney Chris Coffey sought to shift the focus from Tadaryl Shipp to Christa Pike. Conceding that his client had cut the victim, Coffey prompted Dr. Elkins to admit that wounds from the pentagram would not have been fatal to Colleen. He stressed that the blows to the head, blows perpetrated by Christa, were the cause of death, not the slash marks and cuts made by Tadaryl.

The fifteen jurors were sequestered for the night in a secret location known only to the court. Crabtree hoped they had slept well. He planned an explosion of evidence the following day that would include the audio-taped confession of Tadaryl Shipp.

Before taking his seat in court on the third day of testimony, Tadaryl glanced at his mother. His face continued to be void of expression. Emery Charlton managed a faint smile for her only son.

Investigator Randy York took the stand for the prosecution. He related to jurors the condition of the body when he arrived at the crime scene on January 13, 1995, more than two years earlier.

"When I left the crime scene, I proceeded to the University of Tennessee Hospital," York said.

"After the body was cleaned, I observed a diagram on the chest of the victim. It was a circle with an upside-down five-pointed star. The symbol itself represents the goat head, which is the symbol for Satan," York explained.

Tadaryl sat at the defense table, still void of expression.

"Did you release information to the public?" Crabtree asked.

"Absolutely not, just the fact that we had found a body, that the person was dead, and that the police were investigating the murder," York responded.

"I'll show you what has been marked as Exhibit Seventy-One and ask if you recognize that," Crabtree said.

"I do. It is a picture of Tadaryl Shipp, the way he looked the morning when he was brought into the police station for questioning," York answered, looking at the short-haired youth beside his attorney.

Crabtree then showed York another photo, this one of Christa Pike, also taken the morning she was interviewed at the Knoxville Police Department. York acknowledged that, in both the photo of Tadaryl, and the one of Christa, each was wearing a medallion-type necklace. The veteran detective then identified two necklaces presented by Crabtree as those worn by Pike and Shipp in the photos.

The medallions were five-pointed stars, or pentagrams, set in circular mounts on chains. In addition, York identified a second necklace worn by Tadaryl, a turquoise stone set in a silver-toned mounting, along with a hand/claw, both secured on a black cord.

In addition, York recognized a hexagram-shaped earring belonging to Tadaryl, along with a hexagram pin taken from the teen's ball cap.

"What does the hexagram represent?" Crabtree asked.

"In the Jewish religion it represents the Star of David. In the satanic realm, it's the symbol that conjures up or controls demons," York explained.

"What did Tadaryl Shipp call that star?" Crabtree inquired.

"He first stated 'pentagon,' but then 'pentagram.' He also use the term 'satanic star,' " York answered.

York told jurors that he had seen the same pentagram design on a satanic bible found in Tadaryl's room at the Job Corps Center, as well as carved in the bloody chest of Colleen Slemmer.

With York still on the stand, jurors, attorneys, and courtroom observers listened closely as Tadaryl's oral confession was played for the court. The young man accused of the killing explained that, while Colleen Slemmer was lying half-dead on the muddy ground, he decided to carve a five-pointed, upside-down "satanic star" in the victim's chest. "It just came in my mind," Tadaryl could be heard saying.

A hushed quiet fell over the courtroom. Only the sound of the tape-recorded confession broke the tense silence. Jurors remained emotionless, their eyes occasionally glancing at Tadaryl. No one could interpret their impression of the cold, calm statements of the defendant.

On the taped confession, Shipp told York he

had used a box cutter to carve the star, or pentagram, between Colleen's breasts. Then, his girlfriend, Christa Pike, had cut a circle around the star.

"Afterwards, I thought about it being a sacrifice," Tadaryl said, admitting he had been interested in Satan worship for years.

The defendant's interest in the Satanic and the occult played a key role in the prosecutors' case. In his own statement he spoke of worshiping the devil late at night.

Tadaryl acknowledged cutting, hitting, and tripping Colleen during the thirty to sixty minutes she was tortured. However, he denied any knowledge of a plan to kill Colleen. "I thought Christa only wanted to scare her," Tadaryl said. "I'm not happy with what I did."

On cross-examination, Coffey prompted York to acknowledge that Tadaryl had told him he had walked away a couple of times during the attack, because he didn't want to watch what was happening to Colleen. Tadaryl admitted helping Pike dump the body on a pile of refuse, but denied hitting her in the head with asphalt chunks.

"In his statement, Mr. Shipp said that Christa and Shadolla had made a plan to do something to Colleen?" Coffey asked York, attempting to focus jurors' attention back to Christa Pike and Shadolla Peterson.

"I believe that's accurate, yes," York stated.

"He never said that he made a plan to do something to Colleen, did he?" Coffey asked.

"No, not in those words," York answered.

"He said in his statement that Shadolla hit Colleen with her fist. Is that right?" Coffey asked.

"That's correct."

"He said that Shadolla had a box cutter, is that right?" Coffey inquired.

"That's correct," York said flatly.

"He also stated that Shadolla cut her on the chest and on the face across here"—Coffey indicated with a sweep of his hand across his face—"is that right?"

"I believe that's accurate, yes," York answered.

"He also said that she cut her throat several times, is that right?" Coffey persisted.

"That's correct," York said. The handsome detective was excused.

The taped confession was one of the most powerful pieces of evidence prosecutors Helm and Crabtree had to put Tadaryl Shipp in prison for life. They believed Tadaryl Shipp was a vicious and cold-blooded accomplice. They theorized that their next witness would prove it.

Shadolla Renee Peterson entered the courtroom and took the witness stand in front of Tadaryl at the defense table. The young black woman was neatly dressed, with her braided hair tidily tied at the back of her neck. She shifted uneasily as William Crabtree approached the stand.

"How did you know Tadaryl Shipp?" Crabtree asked.

"I used to braid his hair," Shadolla answered softly.

Crabtree carefully walked Shadolla through the events of the evening of January 12, 1995. Near the end of the description of the frenzied beating and slashing of Colleen Slemmer, Shadolla told the court, "When I looked, Tadaryl was gone. When he came back, he had his hands behind his back and then he said, 'Look what I have.' And then that's when he presented the brick, or whatever it was, to Christa."

"Then what happened?" Crabtree urged.

"Christa drug her back down to where she was killed, and Tadaryl hit her with the brick or whatever it was. Then Christa, she finished her off," Shadolla said, dropping her head slightly.

"What was Christa doing?" Crabtree asked.

"She was dancing around her, saying, 'La, la, la, la, la.' Singing and going on," Shadolla said.

"What happened then?"

"Tadaryl told Christa to stop, and she said, 'No. I want to see brains.' And so she hit her with that one last time, and then she said, 'There they go.' Then she took a piece of her skull and said, 'Look what I have. I have a souvenir,' " Shadolla answered softly.

Crabtree asked Shadolla if Tadaryl had mentioned anything about the day of the month after the murder.

"Tadaryl said, 'It's a full moon outside, and you know what that means.' The next day was Friday the thirteenth, and he said that that was his father's birthday. Satan's birthday," Shadolla answered.

Shadolla told the jury that, as she returned to campus with Christa and Tadaryl, they told her not to say anything about what had happened. At that point she didn't know what to think about what had happened on the University of Tennessee campus. She was scared. In shock.

"I believe you entered a plea of guilty to the offense of accessory after the fact, is that correct?" Crabtree asked.

"Yes, it is," Shadolla answered.

"And got what, a six-year sentence?"

"Yes."

"And you are on probation?"

"Yes."

"As far as the testifying, have you ever been offered anything in exchange for your testimony?" Crabtree asked, anticipating the defense's questioning of his witness.

"No."

"Did you have to clean up there at the restroom?" Crabtree asked, referring to the Texaco station where Christa washed away Colleen's blood from her clothing.

"No, I did not," Shadolla said.

"Why not?" Crabtree inquired.

"Because I had no reason to. I didn't do anything," Shadolla answered.

As expected, Mr. Coffey grilled Shadolla on any promises of a reduced sentence that may have been made to her by the prosecution. Shadolla continued to insist that she had testified of her own free will, with no promises made by the state.

Shadolla's testimony had been used to help prove that Tadaryl Shipp had indeed helped in the murder of Christa Pike. The state expected the next two witnesses to aid them in proving their contention that Tadaryl had conspired to commit the murder of Colleen Slemmer. The first to testify was Daniel Wayland, Jr., of Nashville.

Wayland was a student at the Job Corps at the time of the murder and friends with Colleen, Christa, Tadaryl, and Shadolla. He explained that on the night of the murder, he was sitting with friends on a wooden fence near the Job Corps when he spoke with Christa, Tadaryl, and Shadolla.

"Christa asked, 'Have you seen Colleen?'" Wayland testified.

When Wayland told her no, he reported to the court that Tadaryl had said, "When we find her, she's dead."

Wayland's testimony was scrutinized at length by the defense because when he first told police investigators about the statement, he had attributed it to Christa, not Tadaryl.

"What does it say that you said right there?" Coffey asked, handing Wayland a copy of his statement to police during cross-examination.

"'Christa said, "When I find her, she's dead."'" Wayland read.

"And that's what you told Detective Gary Price?" Coffey asked.

"I'm not exactly sure," Wayland said waffling.

"You did not tell Gary Price that Tadaryl said, 'When I find her, she's dead.' Is that right?" Coffey pursued the question.

"If I have to repeat myself because . . . maybe you need a hearing aid, but I said I wasn't exactly sure," Wayland snapped.

"Sir, you will not get smart with the attorney. You will answer the question," Judge Leibowitz instructed him sternly,

"I might need a hearing aid. I'm not sure," Coffey quipped.

"Ask the question, Mr. Coffey," the judge said harshly.

Wayland attempted to explain to the defense his reason for changing his statement.

"I've had two years to sit there and think about what really happened. When a murder happens, your mind goes blank. I don't know if you've ever had someone you know get murdered or not, but it's not the best thing in the world to happen. And your mind isn't exactly working properly for a while. And I have had two years. And since that two years, I've actually thought about what really went on," Wayland said.

Coffey pursued his questioning, implying that Wayland had deliberately changed his story, leaving spectators to consider why he would do such a thing. Was it to see that Tadaryl was punished for the murder of Daniel's friend Colleen? Or was it to get even with Tadaryl for some untold motive?

Kip Mitchell O'Hara followed Wayland's appearance on the stand. Like Wayland, he, too, was a student at the Job Corps in January 1995.

"On Sunday, the week before the murder, did you have a conversation with the defendant?" Crabtree asked.

"Yes, sir. In my room on the second floor. Tadaryl came in with an Ouija board. I told him to get out of my room. He said it was a week that the moon or stars and sun and star faces were in alignment and that he had to make a human sacrifice," O'Hara said.

Coffey was on his feet. "Objection, Your Honor! That's totally irrelevant," Coffey said loudly.

No explanation was made to the jury or the court in regards to Ouija boards. Perhaps Crabtree and Coffey assumed that everyone on the panel knew that a Ouija board was often used to spell out words or sentences, supposedly conveying messages from the spirit world to the players. The popular game, developed in the nineteenth century, is generally made of wood, with letters of the alphabet imprinted along the outer edge. Participants place a finger lightly on a small heart-shaped wooden piece with casters, allowing it to move freely about the board.

Tadaryl's interests in the Ouija board probably came from knowing they are often used in seances or other occult activities.

After several minutes of argument between Coffey and Crabtree, Judge Leibowitz ruled that the testimony would be allowed.

"What occurred after Mr. Shipp had made this statement?" Crabtree asked.

"We talked some more about the Ouija board. I got up. I put the Ouija board in the trash bag, and I took it down to the Dumpster," O'Hara answered.

On cross-examination, Coffey tried to neutralize O'Hara's testimony.

"Mr. Shipp certainly didn't say he was going to kill Colleen Slemmer, is that right?" Coffey asked.

"True."

"He didn't say he was going to kill a Job Corps student, did he?" Coffey asked.

"True."

Crabtree had confirmed Tadaryl's presence at the scene, planted the seed of premeditation, and now he wanted to show that the blood of Colleen Slemmer was on Tadaryl Shipp.

Raymond DePriest of the Tennessee Bureau of Investigation was called to the stand. A serology specialist, DePriest dealt with human body fluids.

DePriest had tested the hooded sweatshirt, Nike sweat pants, and black T-shirt investigators had found in Tadaryl's dorm room after obtaining his consent to search. The reddish-brown stains had tested positive for human blood. It was the blood of Colleen Slemmer.

After all the state's witnesses were presented, it was time for the defense to take center stage in its effort to convince jurors that Tadaryl Shipp had not committed first-degree murder, or conspired to commit first-degree murder.

In a surprise move, Coffey presented no witnesses, only a motion for judgment of acquittal on both charges.

"Your Honor, with respect to the conspiracy count, I would submit that there has been no proof as to Mr. Shipp making any agreement to commit the offense of first-degree murder.

"There has been some testimony that Pike and Peterson were involved in securing the weapons. There had been no indication of that with regard to Mr. Shipp. The only testimony with respect to an agreement to commit the offense is that they all went up there together. I don't think that is enough to show the formation of a conspiracy.

"I think the other element is that each member of the alleged conspiracy has to have the same intent. I don't think that has been shown in this case.

"I think that the proof has been that one person made a decision to kill at the scene that night, and no one else was a party to that decision.

"There is no credible proof as to Mr. Shipp on premeditation.

"The proof has been that he didn't know what was going to happen when he went up there. That Pike and Peterson had planned something, but he wasn't sure what. I think what the proof has been is that Pike had to get herself out of this, and she made a decision to kill. And that no one else was a party to that decision.

"I think there is no question that Christa Pike was the principal. But I don't think there has been any proof that Mr. Shipp's intent was the same as hers. I don't think the conduct of another would pull him into first-degree murder, based on the proof that has been presented. Thank you."

Assistant District Attorney Crabtree's responding argument covered the evidence presented in the case, then concluded with:

"We would submit that there is an abundance of proof here that the jury can find the defendant guilty of the offense of murder in the first degree, and also the offense of conspiracy to commit murder in the first degree, and we would ask the court to so find."

Judge Leibowitz looked confidently at the attorneys from both sides. After adjusting her metal-rimmed glasses, she spoke to the defense.

"Clearly, there has been some sufficient proof of Mr. Shipp's knowledge. What his intent may be is the conclusion of the jury, as well as his level of criminal responsibility. I will allow this case to go to the jury.

"I am going to deny the motion for judgment of acquittal at this time," the judge said firmly. The state was ready to present its final arguments.

Eighteen

Although May Martinez had vowed she wouldn't return to Knoxville, she found herself wanting to face Tadaryl Shipp. She wanted to see him punished for killing Colleen.

With the help of the Florida Victim's Compensation Fund, which paid a portion of her expenses, May was able to reclaim her seat at the front of the Knox County courtroom. She watched closely as Tadaryl entered from the secured corridor.

Tadaryl returned May's glaring stare. His eyes glowed with a redness that May was convinced was an evil fire burning inside him. His steadfast gaze bore through her as if she were transparent. Frightened, May was certain she was watching the devil himself. For an instant, she understood at least a fraction of the fear that must have griped Colleen on that darkened, lonely service road on the night of her death. May felt certain that Tadaryl would kill again, if not convicted.

Jurors had been listening attentively to witnesses and viewing exhibits for three and a half days. Crabtree had warned them in his opening statement, just as he had warned jurors in the Christa Pike case, that what they would see and hear in the courtroom was worse than any nightmare they could imagine. He had been right. As Ms. Helm said in her closing statement, "The most unfortunate part about it is, one person lived that nightmare and died that nightmare, and that was Colleen Slemmer."

May thought of the ordeal she had been living through for two years. Rehearing the details of Colleen's death, seeing her clothes, the photos of her mutilated body, knowing that the killers had no remorse for their evil act. Those dreams danced in her head like paper skeletons at the end of a cord. They haunted her.

Chris Coffey rose from the defense table and slowly walked to the jury box.

"The issue in this case is not whether it was horrendous, or horrible, or awful. The issue in this case is if Tadaryl Shipp is guilty of first-degree murder," Coffey said.

May felt a biting anger in the pit of her stomach. Regardless of what the defense said, the case *was* about the horrendous, horrible, awful murder of her daughter.

"'Everyone knows who killed Colleen Slemmer. That person was Christa Pike, and it is undisputed," Coffey stated.

"Christa Pike picked up the asphalt. Christa Pike crushed her skull. So the issue is, what is Mr. Shipp's level of culpability?" Coffey paused momentarily. He took a deep breath and wiped his eyes. Near tears, Coffey continued.

"This is an emotional case for everyone, especially you. You've seen pictures, clothes, and a lot of things. You've heard five or ten different people talking about what they saw when they got to the scene. I felt that was unnecessary, because it is so emotional. You can't decide this case on emotion. You have to decide based on what happened, without emotion," Coffey said, his voice breaking.

On the issue of conspiracy, Coffey restated his contention that it was Christa Pike and Shadolla Peterson who had planned to harm Colleen. Coffey again claimed Tadaryl didn't know what was going to happen on that dark, isolated roadway.

"There was never an agreement, and no proof that there had been an agreement to kill, intentionally, with premeditation, because Christa Pike made that decision up there," Coffey told jurors.

On the issue of first-degree murder, again Coffey placed the blame entirely on the shoulders of Christa Pike.

"He did some things. Boy, I can't tell you that it's not horrifying," Coffey said. "But it is undisputed that one person killed her.

"Christa had the motive. And it's crazy. She had a motive because it was her boyfriend, and she thought somebody was after her boyfriend."

May shook her head in disgust. She believed Tadaryl indeed had planned, along with Christa, to murder Colleen. Not because of a contrived love triangle, but as a sacrifice to his idol, Satan. Colleen had been an innocent victim of sadistically sick troubled youths.

Coffey's voice changed from being filled with sadness to an edge of anger as he attacked the credibility of witnesses Wayland and O'Hara, the two Job Corps students whose testimony lent credence to the state's contention that the crime was premeditated, and that Tadaryl was an active part of the plan.

"When these guys come in here and start making up stuff, then I have to get up and confront them," Coffey said.

The counselor took a deep breath and began to wind down his closing.

"Am I trying to blame Christa Pike for what Tadaryl Shipp did?" Coffey asked. "No, I'm not. The state is trying to blame what Christa Pike did on him. The state is not trying to hold Shadolla Peterson accountable for what Christa Pike did. Not equal justice," Coffey argued.

May Martinez agreed. She still believed Shadolla had had an active role in the death of Colleen. Tadaryl's oral confession had merely cemented her feeling. Her anger overflowed as she thought of Shadolla being paroled. Free.

"There was one murderer, one first-degree murderer up there that night. I ask you to follow the law and return a verdict of not guilty to first-degree murder. Not guilty of conspiracy to commit first-degree murder. Thank you."

When impassioned Chris Coffey finished his

closing remarks, he sank in the chair next to his client, emotionally spent.

"Ladies and gentlemen, I want to apologize to you for standing up here and probably sounding somewhat like a frog for the last two days," Assistant District Attorney Crabtree said in a gravelly voice.

"If Mr. Coffey's argument is accepted, then it sounds like I need to apologize to the defendant for all these wrongs that he's been done. But I don't think that's appropriate.

"There is one thing that comes from the mouth of that defendant right there"—Crabtree pointed to Tadaryl— "that shows that he did premeditate, and he did deliberate, and he did conspire.

"And what is that one thing?

"That one thing is when he told you, in the statement that he gave to Randy York, about how Colleen Slemmer got up and was running away, and that he got her and brought her back. He brought her back. At the time he brought her back, she had already suffered injuries to her neck.

"Her throat had been cut. Her back had been carved. Her chest had been carved. She had had that rag tied around her throat to keep her quiet. When he brought her back, what did he think was going to happen? That they were going to bind her wounds? Or maybe they were going to sign off on their artwork, the pentagram on her chest.

"He knew what was going to happen. She was going to be killed," Crabtree said in a raised voice.

May looked to Emery Charlton, Tadaryl's mother, who was crying. As with Christa's mother, May found it difficult to sympathize with a mother whose child could spend his life in prison, while her child had received a death sentence at his hands.

"We're talking about a young lady fighting and struggling, and trying to get away. Trying to get away from the people who are killing her.

"How can anyone stand up here and say that by the time these things were happening to her, that when Colleen Slemmer was being sliced and stabbed and cut, that this defendant ever thought that she was going to be allowed to leave there?

"Mr. Coffey wants you to just ignore what Kip O'Hara said about this sacrifice. But remember, the defendant himself told you in his statement about the sacrifice. According to his statement, after killing her, he sacrificed her soul to the devil.

"The star was placed on her before she died, while she was conscious. Do we have living sacrifices? He knew when he put that star on her, she was not going to leave there alive.

"Counsel says, 'Christa Pike did it.' Who rendered the decisive blow? It doesn't matter. The proof shows that this defendant was there, and that he participated and knew what was going on.

"And I submit to you, that when you look at

and consider the entirety of the proof in this case, you will find this defendant, Tadaryl Shipp, guilty of the offense of murder in the first-degree, and that he did conspire with one or more persons to commit the offense of murder in the first degree. Thank you."

Crabtree retired to the prosecution table.

Judge Leibowitz charged the jury with the duty of deliberation, excusing the three alternates, and asking that the remaining six-man, six-woman jury consider Tadaryl Shipp's guilt or innocence.

Three hours later, they returned with a verdict.

Guilty of first-degree murder.

Tadaryl looked back at his mother, as his stepfather wiped tears from Emery's cheeks.

Guilty of conspiracy to commit first-degree murder.

The verdict brought satisfaction to May Martinez.

"He got what he deserved," May told reporters.

Emery Charlton and her husband, Jim, met with Tadaryl as a dejected Chris Coffey left the courthouse.

Coffey had lost the first battle, but there was another war to wage. Although Tadaryl, only seventeen at the time of the murder, could not be given the death penalty, he could face life in prison without the possibility of parole. Coffey had to see that that would not happen. He headed back to his office to begin preparing for another round with Crabtree and Helm.

The following morning, May Martinez was confronted with an all-too-familiar encounter. The mother of the victim was face-to-face with the mother of a killer.

Emery Charlton, a nicely dressed African-American woman with short hair, stood across from May Martinez. The two women, diversely different in appearance, were likewise contrarily positioned on their views of punishment for Tadaryl.

"I'm hoping Tadaryl gets life," Emery told May.

"I hope he gets death. He deserves it," May answered.

Emery's head drooped slightly. She seemed to understand May's feelings. She knew May had lost a daughter, but she didn't want to lose her only son.

May hoped Emery could grasp her hurt, her anger. She wanted Emery to see that she still had her son, and that May had nothing. She wanted Emery to realize that Colleen didn't deserve anything that happened to her because of Tadaryl.

The two women walked somberly into the courtroom.

Emery took the stand, forcing a small smile for Tadaryl. She told the court that she and her husband, Jim, resided in Memphis, Tennessee, where she was a payroll administrator for the Coca-Cola Bottling Company and Jim was an area manager for Nike.

The heartbroken mother told jurors that Tadaryl first attended school in Byhalia, Mississippi, where he lived with his father. Then, at age nine, he went to live with Emery and Jim in Memphis, where he went to Rice Elementary, then Kirby Middle School, and Kirby High School.

"In the first years he was an A student. When he moved with me, he began to be a B, C student," Emery explained.

"In middle school, things started changing. There was a lot of activity going on in that school and I became very concerned because his grades had never been like that before. I talked to the principals, I talked to school administrators, I talked to everybody. I saw a change in him, so I wanted to move him to private school.

"We counseled and counseled with them and they told me that the school that he was in was the best possible school in the city and there was no need to put him in a private school. My fear for Tadaryl was that the gang was after him," Emery said.

Tadaryl's mother's head dropped slightly. She had given the court a thumbnail sketch of her son's troubles, but she hadn't told the jury everything.

Frustrated with Tadaryl's behavior, when Tadaryl was approximately twelve years old, Emery had placed him in Lakeside Hospital in Memphis. Tadaryl never knew why he had been sent to Lakeside, but sometimes he told people he thought it was for schizophrenia. (Although there is no single symptom of schizophrenic behavior, it is considered to be a psychosis characterized by a break from reality, emotional distortion, and visible disturbances in thought and behavior—which often includes language and communication.)

"We looked into the possibility of military school in Alabama. It was very expensive," Emery continued with her testimony.

"We talked to Job Corps, and they gave us this beautiful picture of what it would be like, that he could attend the University of Tennessee. My hope was that my child would get a good education and go on to become somebody one day. We made a decision, because of the financial burden, to send him to the Job Corps," Emery said.

Emery told jurors that Tadaryl left for the Knoxville Job Corps when he was sixteen. It was her understanding that he could complete his GED and then go on to the University of Tennessee to become an engineer. She had never had any correspondence from the Job Corps on how Tadaryl was doing.

"What did you know about his interest in satanism and devils and bibles and pentagrams?" Coffey asked.

"I don't know anything about it. I'm not saying that Tadaryl didn't dabble in that. I don't know that. When Tadaryl was with me, he professed to hold in the Lord Jesus Christ in my church as a Methodist. He went to Sunday School and church with me. That's all I know. All of this talk of Satanism, I don't know anything about it." Emery's words were filled with emotion.

Coffey gave Emery a chance to speak to the jury from her heart.

"My son, I always taught him to tell the truth no matter what. I did not teach him the things that he's accused of. I didn't raise him to do anything like this. Never in my wildest dream—all that I can say is that I just hope you have mercy on him. I think that he has a life to be lived, and I'm begging you to give him that chance." The pain in Emery Charlton's face mirrored the obvious pain in her heart.

William Crabtree approached the witness cautiously. He knew she was a wounded mother who only wanted to see her son one day be released from prison and one day lead a normal life. But it was his job to see that no one was ever hurt by Tadaryl Shipp again.

"Have you talked to Tadaryl about the specifics of the case?" Crabtree asked.

"We've talked, yes, sir," Emery answered.

"Did he tell you what happened?"

"No, he didn't. I heard it in court."

"I'm sure you would agree that the behavior he exhibited, at least from what you've heard from the witness stand, is totally unacceptable?" Crabtree inquired.

"Yes, sir."

Emery Charlton left the witness stand. Her teary eyes met her son's blank stare.

Tadaryl Shipp's mother may have wanted to believe that her son was suitable for the engineering program at the University of Tennessee. Tests administered to Tadaryl by Dr. Leonard M. Miller, while he awaited trial in the Knox County Jail, indicated that the troubled youth had a verbal IQ of 95, a performance IQ of 86, and full-scale IQ of 90. This left him in the lower portion of the average range.

During the testing, Tadaryl had demonstrated rather poor judgment and communicative skills, but his reasoning was well within normal limits. He showed impaired verbal expression and limited vocabulary. He was easily distracted.

Personality tests indicated that Tadaryl was in good contact with reality and did not show any indication of a thought disorder or pervasive mood disorder. He didn't handle strong emotional feelings very well or very effectively, and, in spite of his use of rather sophisticated defenses at various times, he fell back on very primitive defense mechanisms when confronted with any emotionally laden situations.

Tadaryl was the kind of person who would utilize avoidance, denial, and withdrawal as a means of dealing with stress. His tests indicated that he didn't effectively think through cause and effect before responding.

That lack of rationally thinking through cause and effect had helped put him before the jury that would consider his punishment for helping to kill Colleen Slemmer.

Ms. Helm again began the closing arguments,

as she had done in the Christa Pike trial, with an explanation of the two aggravating factors:

> *(1) The murder was especially heinous, atrocious, or cruel in that it involved torture or serious physical abuse beyond that necessary to produce death.*
> *(2) The murder was committed for the purpose of avoiding, interfering with, or preventing a lawful arrest, prosecution of the defendant or another.*

Helm finished her plea for conviction of Tadaryl Shipp for first-degree murder with explosive rhetoric.

"They didn't take a gun and put it to her head and 'Boom!' that was it," Helm said with great inflection. "They tortured her. They chased her down. They branded her. And when all else failed, they crushed her skull."

The courtroom was silent. Helm had made an impassioned plea for guilt. The defense would have a tough hill to climb to overcome the prosecution's fervent closing.

Chris Coffey approached the jury for the final time in defense of Tadaryl Shipp.

"The proof in this case has been absolutely and totally that Christa Pike was scared she was going to get caught. There has been no proof with regard to Mr. Shipp, that that's why this happened—to avoid getting caught," Coffey said, addressing the state's second aggravating factor.

Coffey offered mitigating circumstances which he asked the jury to consider while deliberating punishment. They included that the defendant had no history of prior criminal activity; that the defendant was an accomplice in the murder committed by another person and his participation was relatively minor; the youthfulness of the defendant at the time of the crime; and any other mitigating factors raised by the proof presented in the case.

"This case is a tragedy. It is a tragedy for Ms. Slemmer, Ms. Slemmer's family.

"It is a tragedy for Mr. Shipp's family.

"Tadaryl's mother has faith that maybe her son, because of the way she brought him up, can come out one day and do something right.

"He's going to have a long time to think about what he did. And she can live to see him one day get out, maybe," Coffey said.

May Martinez's eyes narrowed as she glared at the defense attorney. Why should Emery Charlton live to see her son released from prison? She would never see Colleen again.

"The state is going to get up and say, 'What about Ms. Slemmer? She didn't have another chance,' " Coffey stated.

"But that doesn't change that, maybe, if a human being has done wrong, incredibly wrong, that some day he can do something productive.

"He's got the foundation for it. He's gone off track somewhere. Think about that, and don't make the tragedy any worse than it is.

"If he gets life in prison, that doesn't mean that he automatically gets out. That means that he has the opportunity, maybe, someday to get out.

"I thank you for your attention," Coffey said in closing.

Crabtree approached the jury. It was familiar territory. It was the same courtroom where he had secured a death sentence for Christa Pike. He was prepared to ask this jury to send Tadaryl Shipp to prison for the rest of his life.

"Tadaryl Shipp's statement was introduced. His version of what occurred. I think it's obvious, from reading that statement, what he was trying to do. He was trying to dump on somebody else. Yet he had to explain the blood on his clothing, and things of that nature. So he made a couple of statements in there about his participation.

"Can there be any doubt at all that what this defendant has been convicted of was cruel, heinous, and atrocious? Isn't this the definition of torture?

"They slashed her throat. She was still alive. So to make sure she can't report anything, asphalt was taken to her head. And she's beaten until her brains show," Crabtree said.

Those who attended both the trials of Pike and Shipp had heard this argument for punishment before. The graphic description of the slaying. The reference to the victim's brains spilling from her skull. Reporters and spectators alike were ready for the trial to end. Ready to put behind them the verbal illustration painted by the prosecutors that would be forever embedded in their minds.

"Also keep in mind, we are not trying the defendant's mother. She's not the one that has been charged with these crimes. She is not the one who committed these crimes. That man over there is the one who committed these offenses," Crabtree said, pointing to Tadaryl.

"From what you've heard here can any of you ever rest easy thinking that that man, someone who did what he did, would ever be released on society?" Crabtree asked in conclusion.

May Martinez shuddered. The thought of Tadaryl released in society kept her awake at night, even after she'd been prescribed tranquilizers to help her sleep. Despite medication, the image of Tadaryl continued to race through her mind—continued to spook her.

Judge Leibowitz, from her bench above the courtroom, addressed the jury. "It is now your duty to determine, within the limits prescribed by law, the penalty which shall be imposed as punishment for this offense.

"Tennessee law provides that a person convicted of murder in the first degree shall be punished by imprisonment for life without possibility of parole, or by imprisonment for life," Judge Leibowitz instructed them.

The jury retired to the jury room to deliberate. May Martinez and Emery Charlton roamed the City-County Building awaiting word of a decision.

Emery Charlton cautiously, but with purpose, approached May Martinez. In a sincere though shaky voice, Emery apologized to May for what happened to her daughter. A few words were exchanged, then the two grieving mothers parted.

The twelve-person jury returned from the jury room and their final deliberation.

"We, the jury, unanimously agree that the defendant shall be sentenced to imprisonment for life," jury foreman William Blair announced.

"Is that the verdict of each and every juror?" Judge Leibowitz asked. "Signify by raising your hand."

All twelve jurors raised their hand to be counted by the judge.

"Not fair," May could be heard saying softly. "Not fair at all."

Shipp would have to serve at least twenty-five years before he could be considered for release. But the imposed sentence was a victory for Chris Coffey.

"I think they decided that maybe it's not worth throwing a life away because of another life," Coffey said.

May Martinez strongly disagreed. Colleen's life was worth far more than a mere twenty-five years. In twenty-five years, Emery Charlton could hold her child.

In twenty-five years May would still feel the void left by Colleen's death—a void that could never be filled.

Epilog

CHRISTA GAIL PIKE is currently on death row at the Tennessee Prison for Women in Nashville for the murder of Colleen Slemmer.

Dozens of news organizations from around the world have beaten a path to Pike's jail cell. The first was Charley Belcher of WATE-TV in Knoxville. Among the others have been the national news program *Fox Files* and *Death Row Magazine.*

Pike's defense attorneys believed the publicity could benefit their client, hoping it would refresh Christa's cold, calculating, murderous image. The attorneys hoped that her youth and gender would help in eventually having her death sentence commuted.

"Anyone who knows me understands that the person convicted of killing Colleen was not the real Christa Pike. Maybe no one else will forgive me, but I think the Lord will stand by me," Christa said tearfully in her interview with Belcher.

Viewers and readers have seen a different side of Christa Pike. Not the demon devil-worshiper convicted of brutally killing Colleen Slemmer, but a frail, remorseful young girl moved to tears by a senseless impulse. The remorseful image fades quickly when photos of the gruesome death are exposed. Viewers and readers are soon reminded of the Christa Pike who tortured Slemmer, taunted her, and ultimately caused her death.

In November 1997, the Tennessee State Court of Criminal Appeals affirmed Christa Gail Pike's murder conviction and death sentence. Because it's a death-penalty case, Christa has an automatic right of appeal to the Tennessee Supreme Court.

The first European settlers in America accepted the death penalty as just punishment for a variety of offenses. The English Penal Code listed fourteen capital offenses, but the actual offenses varied from colony to colony. In the Massachusetts Bay Colony, thirteen crimes warranted the death penalty: idolatry, witchcraft, blasphemy, rape, statutory rape, kidnapping, perjury in a trial involving a possible death sentence, rebellion, murder, assault in sudden anger, adultery, and buggery (sodomy). In the statute each crime was accompanied by an appropriate biblical quotation justifying the capital punishment. Arson, treason, and grand larceny were later added. Today only those found guilty of capital murder face the death penalty.

Only time will tell when or if Christa Pike will be executed for her heinous crime. Since the reinstatement of the death penalty by the U.S. Supreme Court in 1976, only two men and no women have died by the executioner's hand in Tennessee. Although dozens of men have met death in execution chambers across America, only three women have been executed to date: Velma Barfield on November 2, 1984, in Florida; Karla Fay Tucker on February 3, 1998, in Texas; and Judias Buenoana on March 3, 1998, in Florida.

Christa lives in an eight-foot-by-ten-foot cell adorned with paper butterflies and angel trinkets. She is confined to the cell twenty-three hours a day. She is allowed one hour for outside exercise. Christa's meals are passed through a slot in the cell's gray steel door. Her only communication is with a young woman nextdoor—they talk through the electrical outlet.

A photo of Karla Faye Tucker, the first woman to be executed in Texas in the twentieth century, rests on the top of Christa's private television set. "I just love her. She was so changed. So sweet," Christa said of Karla Faye, a pick-ax murderer and drug addict who had accepted Christ and married the prison chaplain while awaiting her date with the executioner.

It has been reported that Christa and a county music promoter have agreed to marry. The man, who has never met Christa, saw her on television and began corresponding with the convicted killer. Their plans to unite in marriage were crushed when it was discovered that he was a convicted felon and was therefore denied prison visits.

When it is time for Christa Pike to be executed

for the murder of Colleen Slemmer, she will be transferred to a death watch cell for her four remaining days. There will be no special last meal, only what is regularly planned on the prison menu.

"I'm not scared to die. I'm scared of being shocked to death," Christa said of dying by electrocution.

Two thousand, six hundred and forty volts of electricity would have run through Christa's body if she'd been strapped into the electric chair that inmates call "Old Sparky." But Tennessee law changed, phasing out electrocution in January 1999. Christa has opted to die by the lethal injection of a deadly combination of drugs.

No one knows, including Christa herself, how she will handle the final minutes before her death. Perhaps she will follow the example of her model, Karla Fay Tucker. Tucker, who did not fear death, was reported to have hopped on the gurney and pray, "Jesus, please help them find my vein." She spoke to the families of her victims of forgiveness and regret and said she prayed that God would give them peace.

Christa's execution is not likely to occur anytime soon. Tennessee hasn't executed an inmate since November 1960, a fact that infuriates May Martinez, who is upset that while many people struggle to eat, Christa Pike enjoys three meals a day.

"I don't feel the taxpayers' money should go to keep her alive," May said. "Why should she have the privilege to live?"

May will have to continue to wait for the death of her daughter's killer. Meanwhile, Christa continues to grant interviews.

"I can't pinpoint where my life went off track, where I went wrong. Nothing at all in life is worth where I am now," Christa said in a recent interview.

TADARYL SHIPP is currently serving his life sentence in the Southeast Correctional Institution in Pikeville, Tennessee. Shortly after receiving his punishment, Judge Leibowitz sentenced him to an additional twenty-five years for the conspiracy to commit murder conviction.

The maximum sentence was levied in spite of a letter from Garry Tener, Minister to Prisons, Beech Grove Baptist Church, Louisville, Tennessee. Tener wrote Judge Leibowitz that Tadaryl had made a good start toward positive spiritual development, having professed his faith in Jesus Christ and been baptized. Tener's letter carried little weight with the strong-willed judge.

"There is no doubt that at this time Mr. Shipp is a dangerous man and has no regard for human life," Leibowitz said, noting his interest in Satanism.

The sentences, which will run consecutively, will leave Shipp eligible for parole when he is fifty-two.

Tadaryl has maintained contact with Christa, through letters.

* * *

SHADOLLA PETERSON is living in Cleveland, Tennessee. She now has two children. Shadolla was in jeopardy of losing her probation and being sent to prison for her six-year term as an accessory after the fact in the brutal slaying of Colleen Slemmer. The young mother had failed for several months to report to her probation officer and was behind in paying her court fees. Judge Leibowitz gave Peterson a stern warning and a second chance to comply with the terms of her probation. Peterson's probationary period will be completed in 2002.

MAY AND RAUL MARTINEZ continue to reside in Florida with their young daughter. May believes she will not have any closure in the death of Colleen as long as she is unable to reclaim the skull of her daughter. While Christa Pike pursues an appeal of her conviction, the skull of Colleen Slemmer remains a key piece of evidence and is maintained with the case file. Until Christa's execution, the skull cannot be returned to Colleen's grieving mother.

May filed a lawsuit against Career Systems, who operated the Knoxville Job Corps, in Knox County Circuit Court. She sought up to three million dollars in punitive damages and up to three million dollars in compensatory damages for the death of her daughter. May alleged that Career Systems was motivated by the money it received for recruiting Corps students. She asserted that the operator allowed students who posed a threat to the safety of others to live at the center. The suit was eventually dropped.

When six prisoners escaped a Tennessee prison in 1998, May called to verify that Tadaryl Shipp was not one of the escapees. She still fears Tadaryl.

May continues to have nightly nightmares. She will awaken, thinking Colleen is outside. She clings to her youngest daughter and prays that no harm will come to her. May has lost all trust in mankind.

In memory of Colleen, May and Raul planted a rose garden at their Jacksonville, Florida, home. Roses were Colleen's favorite flower.

May and Raul plan to attend the execution of Christa Pike, whenever it takes place.

RANDY YORK retired from the Knoxville Police Department and is currently a court officer in Judge Mary Beth Leibowitz's court.

WILLIAM TALMAN, Christa's court-appointed attorney, was cited by the court for overbilling legal fees payable by the state. His fee for appealing Christa's death-penalty conviction was cut nearly in half, from $9,855 to $5,000. In 1995, Talman reimbursed the state about $60,000 after an audit found he had charged too much to represent clients in court-appointed cases, such as Christa's. There were times when he had billed more than twenty-four hours in a day.

WILLIAM CRABTREE continues to serve in the Knox County District Attorney General's office as the most senior prosecutor.

CHARLEY BELCHER is now a news reporter for the Fox television station in Tampa, Florida.

JOHN NORTH continues to cover the courts in Knoxville, Tennessee for the *Knoxville News-Sentinel*, where he is consistently recognized for his fine work.